WILD NIGHTS

Conversations with Mykonos About Passionate Love,

Extraordinary Sex, and How to Open to God

DAVID DEIDA

PLEXUS
2000

IMPORTANT CAUTION - PLEASE READ THIS

Although anyone may find the practices, disciplines and understandings in this book to be useful, it is made available with the understanding that neither the author nor the publisher are engaged in presenting specific medical, psychological, emotional, sexual, relational, or spiritual advice. Nor is anything in this book intended to be a diagnosis, prescription, recommendation, or cure for any specific kind of medical, psychological, emotional, sexual, relational, or spiritual problem. Each person has unique needs and this book cannot take these individual differences into account. Each person should engage in a program of treatment, prevention, cure, or general health only in consultation with a licensed, qualified physician, therapist, or other competent professional. Any person suffering from venereal disease or any local illness of his or her sexual organs or prostate gland should consult a medical doctor and a qualified instructor of sexual yoga before practicing the sexual methods described in this book.

PLEXUS
PMB 445, 815-A Brazos St.
Austin, TX 78701
© 2000 by David Deida

All rights reserved. No part of this book may be reproduced in any form or by any means, electronic or mechanical, including photocopying, recording, or by any information storage and retrieval system, without permission in writing from the publisher.

SPECIAL PRE-PUBLICATION EDITION

Preface

Although I have changed some details—including people, places, and times—the events recorded in this book are essentially true. Mykonos is a real person, and as of this writing, he is still alive. He has always preferred anonymity and truth to publicity and facts, and so it is here.

DD
January 2000

Contents

	Foreword by Gabriel Cousens M.D.	vi
1	The Red Realm	1
2	Wild Night	15
3	Thimble	51
4	Blue Truth	62
5	Beyond Bondage	77
6	She Comes in Two	90
7	Love's Wound	108
8	Being Claimed	130
9	Two White Doves	137
10	Letting Go	147
11	Big Waves	165
12	Cats and Dogs	180
13	Burden of Bliss	195

Foreword by Gabriel Cousens M.D.

Wild Nights by David Deida presents us with a spiritual challenge. This book dares us to open ourselves to the fullest expression of Divine Love in every single moment with every being and every thing. The tantalizing proposition of this book is: Are we willing to be ecstatically and fearlessly present within our everyday experience? Are we willing to keep our hearts open to be continuously consumed by the "Laughing Mama?" Are we willing to choose to continuously make love with the Divine One?

In *Wild Nights*, David makes brilliant use of our society's focus on sexuality as a medium to inspire us, "to be smithereened in bliss, opened beyond all limits, loved absolutely, to give of ourselves completely to infinity." David plays joyfully, powerfully, and masterfully with his teacher's message, at a level of spiritual clarity that is awesome. With finesse, David Guides us into the experience "where fuck becomes more than sex, where it becomes the pulse of God."

As with the Medieval Kabbalahists and the Sufi poetry of Kabir and Hafiz, where sex is a metaphor for opening to the Divine dance, this book exposes us to the experience of Kashmir Shavism, or the Truth of Tantra. We are taken far deeper than the genital location, to the fearless state of vulnerability where we are penetrated by God in every moment. We are led beyond the illusion of doing self-improvement and Tantric techniques, to the surrendered, unlimited, direct state of being the Ultimate Truth in every moment.

Wild Nights is a radically effective work that can arouse a shift of consciousness in a way that knocks on the doors of Liberation. Beyond the fear of death and the fear of life, we begin to pulse with the scintillating, synchronous non-dual / dual play of consciousness in every moment. We open to Life and Love in every breath. This creates the mind space where we die into the infinite openness of the total, uninhibited, raw Truth. The answer to David's dare is: Yes, we *can* be fully present, with our hearts available, continuously choosing to make love with the Divine One. For those who are ready, this book propels us into the final leap of faith, beyond the frontier of the mind, into the pulsating, ecstatic silent That- where all illusions are stripped away and we dance naked with God.

–Gabriel Cousens, M.D., September, 2000

Author: *Spiritual Nutrition and the Rainbow Diet*
and *Conscious Eating*, Revised 2000
Director: Tree of Life Rejuvenation Center

1
The Red Realm

∽

"Hello, my friend," Mykonos said when I opened the door, answering his knock.

He stood outside my cabin, grinning a horse's smile, wearing shorts and a tank top.

"Hi," I said, welcoming Mykonos into my small home. "Come on in."

The one-room beach cabin had no furniture. Mykonos stepped inside, looked around the room for a moment, and sat on the wood floor.

"I didn't expect to see you, Mykonos."

"Well, I just thought I'd stop in. Is that OK?"

"Of course. I'm just surprised that you're here."

I had met Mykonos twice before. The first time was a few years earlier, after Mykonos had been ousted by his spiritual teacher and shunned by his fellow students who he had, supposedly, threatened to beat with a baseball bat.

Then, a week before his appearance at my cabin door, I ran into Mykonos on the beach. We sat together and talked about God, who Mykonos called the "Great One." We watched women walk by, and Mykonos expounded on the spiritual capacity of women's genitals, which stunned me.

When I joked that he seemed obsessed with women, he said, "What would you rather consider besides sex and death?" Not much, I admitted, and Mykonos nodded slightly, looking deep into my eyes. For a moment, everything stopped—no sounds, no motion, even my breath stopped—and then Mykonos got up to go. From the beach, I pointed out my cabin to Mykonos, but I never expected him to actually show up.

"Do you have any cold ones?" Mykonos asked, looking toward my refrigerator.

I figured he wanted a beer. But I didn't have any beer. I didn't drink. My life was very strict. I did three to five hours of spiritual practices in my little cabin every day, and I was a die-hard vegetarian.

"I don't have any beer," I told him.

For a few minutes, Mykonos made some small talk and then got up and left. I regretted that I didn't have any beer to offer him. I knew that Mykonos had a lot to offer me.

Mykonos was a man as ugly as he was tough. I had heard that he grew up on the streets, playing hockey, boxing, and getting into more than his share of trouble. He was also a decorated Vietnam veteran. After recovering from nearly fatal battle wounds, Mykonos, still a very young man, turned from the world and wholly devoted himself to spiritual growth. He spent twenty years studying at the feet of his spiritual teacher before being kicked out, ending up in the same coastal town where I lived.

I knew that he spoke from an enormous wealth of spiritual knowledge—what I didn't know is that he walked his talk with a vengeance, and that he was about to walk into my life and change it forever.

The next time Mykonos showed up at my cabin door, I was prepared. A six-pack waited in the refrigerator.

Mykonos came in and sat on the floor. He seemed particularly animated.

"Do you have any cold ones, my friend?" he asked.

I went to the refrigerator, secretly smiling, and grabbed two cans. One for me, one for him. I handed Mykonos a beer and sat down in front of him. He popped the top and raised the beer high.

"To the Great One," he toasted.

"To the Great One," I replied.

We both took a sip. I couldn't believe it. I was drinking beer. In my spiritual efforts to live a healthy life, I viewed alcohol as poison. But I had to trust Mykonos. If he wanted to drink beer with me, then there must be a reason. I was willing to go along with him and find out.

He took out a pack of cigarettes and lit one. I swallowed. Cigarettes? I had been pure for so long. I hadn't eaten meat, or even drank tea, for more than fifteen years. I didn't want to throw away years of devout purity for a few hours of chatting with a guy who looked like a cross between an ax murderer and a car wash attendant. Mykonos was not a big man, though you wouldn't want to mess with him. Between his knees and his shorts, scars from shrapnel wounds crisscrossed the flesh of his thighs. He had a certain look in his eyes, as if he knew death—from both sides.

As soon as he lit up his cigarette, I was sure Mykonos felt my fear and resistance. He placed the pack within my reach and nodded toward it, indicating that I could help myself. I didn't.

Mykonos took a long drag on his cigarette, and then exhaled very slowly. Smoke filled the room of my clean cabin. He took another sip from his can of beer.

"Ah yesss," Mykonos sighed. "The lady is all around us." He made a sweeping gesture with his hand as if to indicate the beach, or maybe the entire world, outside my cabin. "She is beautiful, is she not? And she'd just as soon kill you. Eat you alive. What a bitch. What a beautiful bitch. Do you have any idea what I am talking about?"

Startled by his vulgar language, I nodded, hoping he would tell me more.

We both continued drinking beer in silence. I waited. Then Mykonos spoke of seemingly random things: books, sports, schemes to make money. I felt he was testing me. Seeing if I would bite. Finding out if I was ready to receive what he had to give, or whether I would be satisfied with small talk and common chat.

Meanwhile, I was starting to feel the effects of the alcohol. By then we had each drank three beers. Having been a long-time teetotaler, I was beginning to spin a little bit. I was losing the thread of the conversation.

"Breathe it down, my friend. Suck her down your front. Breathe her down to here," Mykonos said, firmly grabbing his crotch, which frightened me. "Why separate yourself from her? Hmmm? Why not take it to her? She wants you. She's gonna get you one way or another. She's gonna chew you up when you die. And after you die? On the other side? She's waiting for you there, too. You can't escape her, my friend."

Mykonos took another drag off his cigarette. I was wordless. Reeling.

"No amount of your so-called spiritual practice can save you from her," Mykonos continued. "You can't get away. You can only love. You can live in fear, or you can dance with her. And when you love her without holding back, when you see her as she really is, through and through, she dies in bliss. You know? Only bliss. But if you can't get her to spread her legs, if you won't even drink a beer, if you are too uptight to breathe her down to here, then she's just gonna laugh at you. We are talking about a *big lady*. A *very* big lady. Your agenda doesn't mean shit to her."

As he spoke, I felt dizzy, and my gut tensed. His words were crude, but he was right. I had equated spiritual practice with squelching my desires, denying them, suppressing them. I could sit in a clean room by myself and meditate for hours, but I wouldn't dance with what Mykonos called "the lady." I was afraid of life. I was afraid of death. I was afraid even to drink a beer and lose my purity.

I wanted refuge, not chaos. I wanted peace, not passion. I was trapped in my little room of sanctity, in my meditative stillness and solitude. This wasn't true freedom. Nor was it love. As Mykonos pointed out, I wasn't penetrating the world with my love and opening "her" into bliss. Rather, I was pulling back. I was obsessed with myself.

Maybe the beer was loosening me up, or maybe it was just the right time, but as Mykonos spoke, my entire life strategy began to unravel. I had believed that by keeping my body balanced and my mind clear, then everything would work out. But meanwhile, I was dying anyway. The "lady" was eating me. The whole world was a massive, chaotic woman who terrified me, so I tried to seek safety and refuge in my spiritual inwardness and purity.

"What is a vagina, anyway?" Mykonos suddenly queried. "A lotus of delight or an ugly cut of mucous? Why do you want to poke it so bad? You like to see it in bed, all prettied up, but do you want it as bad when it's on the toilet, shit coming out of the ass? Hmmm? The body is what it is. Usually you like to hide it behind your underwear. You keep the bathroom door closed. Genitals!" Mykonos laughed. "They can be beautiful or disgusting. It's no big deal either way. Love has nothing to do with all that. And, believe me, the big lady doesn't give a damn about your genitals one way or another. If you are going to love the big lady, it's going to take a lot more than your pecker. And the same goes for loving your woman."

I thought of Gia, who was going to college, and wouldn't be able to join me at the beach for several months.

Mykonos smiled and lit another cigarette. Then he offered the pack to me. This time I took a cigarette, put it between my lips, flicked the lighter, and inhaled. The sharpness of the smoke caught me off guard, but I managed to quell my cough. I took a sip of beer, a drag off my cigarette, and tried to relax into the situation.

When we finished the last beer we walked down to the local store to get some more. Then we went to the beach. We sat on the sand, drinking and talking.

Mykonos tilted his head toward a gorgeous blonde tourist walking by in a bikini. I saw smooth tanned skin, narrow waist, and full hips. I saw upright breasts and nipples showing through the fabric of her bikini top. I saw legs to die for. I felt Mykonos regarding me.

"You know what she is?" Mykonos asked with a smile. "Years of arguments, snotty-nosed children, mortgages, and bad smell. You look at that thing every day, day after day, and you just want to run. You know what I mean?"

I did know what he meant, but I didn't say anything. I thought he was talking a little too loudly.

At that moment, we saw another woman walking on the beach. She was about 35 years old, dressed in jeans and a T-shirt. She was a friend that Mykonos and I both happened to know. She was a good person—though, to my taste, she wasn't particularly attractive. I certainly wouldn't call her sexy. She walked up to us and said hi.

"Hello, ma!" Mykonos responded fervently. I assumed that Mykonos developed this habit of speech from spending time in India, where, as a matter of love and respect, women are sometimes referred to as "ma," living facets of the Great Mother, the Goddess of the Universe.

"You are looking very happy today, ma!" Mykonos said.

"I'm doing OK," said the woman, with a shrug.

"You are looking very beautiful. Very radiant. Would you like to have a beer and share the shine of your heart with us, ma?" Mykonos asked her.

"Sure," she said, already visibly happier. And definitely more attractive.

I realized that Mykonos's manner, as outrageous as it seemed, was revealing the limits I put on love. When a woman entranced me, his words disillusioned me. When I was indifferent to a woman, his words unveiled her beauty. Either way, I was trapped by the caprice of my desire, and Mykonos's words, as crass as they were, showed the possibility to open in a way I had never allowed—to offer love without holding back in fear.

"Have either of you ever really been fucked? I mean, *really* fucked," Mykonos asked us.

Before we could respond, he answered his own question. Looking at us, drawing back his lips to expose his front teeth, he shook his head and said, "I don't think so."

He sat in silence, gazing at the ocean. I waited for him to continue, but he didn't. I felt I had to say something.

"Mykonos, what does it mean to be really fucked?" I asked.

He sat for several more minutes without answering, smoking his cigarette, looking out over the water, as if remembering another time and place. Eventually he looked at our friend and smiled.

"Ma knows what fuck is all about. Don't you, ma? Hmmm?"

She grinned, a little shy, a little hesitant to admit it, but definitely like she knew exactly what Mykonos was talking about. He continued.

"You know what it's like to take the Great One so far into you there's nothing left to do but give it all up to the Lord, don't you? Maybe you've never done it. But you know what it would be like. You can feel it. You know you want it. You want to be fucked into God, don't you? Do you know what I mean, ma?"

Now she was smiling, beaming, nodding her head. Mykonos went on.

"Sure you do, ma. You know what it's like because you *are* love. Your heart is love. Your mind is love. Your pussy is love." As he spoke Mykonos looked at her heart, her head, and between her legs. The expression on his face was one of blatant veneration, but without the slightest hint of pretense. I couldn't believe that Mykonos was looking at her crotch this way, without guile and full of virtue and love. Meanwhile, she seemed to be drinking in his praise, basking in his adoration of her form.

"Our poor friend here," Mykonos said, nodding toward me, "He is afraid to fuck. He is afraid to dance with the lady, ma. He wants to stand back and watch, like a scientist. He's afraid to leave his room, to lose his purity and peace that he has worked so hard to attain. He's afraid to lose his precious stillness. He's afraid of the wildness of woman. Everything has to be all tidy for him. He wants the pussy, but he doesn't want the slop. He wants the tit, but not the tooth. Oh, he is a good man, alright. Look at the light in his eyes."

Mykonos put his arm around her shoulders and sat back so both of them could look at me.

"The light has guided his entire life. This boy might just make it. But not until he learns to embrace the lady, ma."

Then, the air around us shifted. A dense rapture grew down upon us, descending into our bodies as thick love, permeating us, impregnating us and the space between us with a blissful pressure. Mykonos continued to speak, his craggy face glowing in beatitude. He began addressing our friend as if she *were* the big lady. He began speaking to her as the Goddess.

"Our boy here won't know love absolute, he won't know what real freedom is, until he can fuck you, and be fucked by you, so that only the Great One shines in his place. And I'm not talking about him wiggling his pecker in your pussy, you know? I'm talking about the heart." Mykonos stroked his heart and the pressure of love seemed to grow. He continued speaking, so tenderly.

"Can you feel it now, ma? Can you breathe love into your pussy? Can you open yourself to the Great One now? Can you feel the Great One everywhere, between your legs, filling your body, breaking your heart wide open?"

Mykonos was looking into her eyes as she began to weep and tremble. Her legs opened and closed as she breathed deeply and gasped, "Yes." Then, more loudly, as her body brightened, she began laughing, without care, full of power, full of sex, full of love. "Yes!" she yelled, ecstatically, fearlessly. She seemed bigger than life, touching herself, opening herself, laughing, radiating fierce energy. Mykonos was right. I was afraid.

"And you, my friend," Mykonos turned to me. "You're going to die anyway. She's going to eat you, sooner or later. Stop struggling. Give it all up now. Give all your love. I mean *all* your love. Why not? What do you think you can gain by holding back? Do you love this woman right now? Can you feel her? Is she not the Goddess? Is she not alive as love unbound?"

She was. Radiant. Open. Alive. Laughing and weeping. Displaying her womanhood without inhibition or pride. Free in her glory. Legs open. Tongue thrust out. Her eyes were wild, full, sexy, unafraid, knowing. She was everything I ever wanted in a woman. Even though I was still afraid, my heart went toward her. My whole body filled with force. The force of desire.

"That's it," Mykonos said to me. "Don't hold back. Don't be an asshole. Love this woman. Give her everything. Feel it all and be free in love. Be open as love. There is only love. Only this Great One, always love, always making love. The Great One is Fuck! There, have I said it? Have I gone too far? There is only the Great One, even in all our seeming twoness."

As outrageous as his words were, Mykonos was right. We were sitting on the beach, fully clothed, not even touching each other, opening as man and woman, alive as love, opening as love, giving love. It was as fuck as fuck gets. And it was clear that every moment was as deeply loving and spontaneously alive as this moment, if we would only consented to give and receive love without holding back or closing down.

"There is only love," Mykonos continued. "There is only this Great One, always churning as love, always making love. Ours isn't a world of angel wings and white spires. Maybe when you die and go to the other side, you'll flit around as golden light. But that's not how love shines in this human realm. Here, in this place of hot blood and rosy flesh, the Great One makes love through bodies of desire. This is the red realm. And the only way beyond it is to feel through it—by loving *as* it."

2
Wild Night

I had moved into a larger home that I was renting. Mykonos arrived early in the evening. He was wearing shorts and a tank top, his eyes shining from the crag of his face, which looked as old and weathered now as it had 30 years earlier in photos he showed me of his time in Vietnam. He still had that intense look in his eyes he called being "on patrol." Mykonos was always on patrol. The Vietnam War had been over for a long time, but for Mykonos, the "holy war" of spiritual life, as he called it, continued.

"Do you have any sake?" he asked.

I didn't, but I knew a nearby liquor store that probably carried the Japanese beverage. By now, I was no longer afraid of drinking alcohol. I used to pride myself on health and purity, meditating every day on a special cushion in a sacred spot reserved in my house for spiritual practices. Now—thanks to the teachings of Mykonos—whether I was sober or drunk, on the beach or in a bar, every moment was an equal opportunity to practice opening to the Great One. We had spent a lot of time together, and I had grown to trust the scurrilous and impure ways of Mykonos's madness.

"I'll go to the store and get some sake," I said.

When I returned home, after buying more than I thought we'd ever use, Mykonos showed me how to heat sake in a pot of water on the stove. Up until now, we had only drunk beer.

"Sake should be as warm as the skin on the inside of a woman's wrist," he informed me.

When the sake reached the proper temperature, we began drinking.

Looking deeply into my eyes, Mykonos raised his glass and toasted, "To the Great One."

"To the Great One," I replied.

"Why don't you invite some of your friends over to drink sake with us?" Mykonos asked.

Mykonos was not a social person, so I was surprised by his invitation. I made a few phone calls to my closest friends that I thought were primed—most had been involved in spiritual practices for a long time and were eager to meet Mykonos—and invited them to the house. I had been getting together with Mykonos for almost a year by myself, and I was excited and a little nervous at this opportunity for Lemuel, Paco, Zelda, and Layla to encounter Mykonos.

Mykonos and I drank and talked at the kitchen table, waiting for everyone to arrive.

"Your friends—do they like sake?" Mykonos asked.

"They'll drink with you, Mykonos." I actually doubted any of them had tasted sake before.

"Too bad most people are afraid to let go of their thinking mind and feel beyond to what is greater, to love," Mykonos said. "Resistance to love is pretty strong. Drugs and alcohol and sex—such sacraments can serve to relax your mind and help open you to the Great One. Of course, they can also relax your mind and turn you into an oinking pig. It all depends on whether you open out to the Great One or in to your own impulses."

"To the Great One," I said, raising my glass.

Mykonos raised his glass silently. He looked serious.

When his glass was empty, I refilled it along with my glass. Every time Mykonos drank, I drank. When he spoke, I listened.

"This place," Mykonos nodded his head toward the whole world, "is not really a place in the physical sense. It is a vision, a realm. Everything you see here, all of your experience, is taking place inside of a *room*."

He looked into my eyes. His eyes seemed endless, so deep and black. When he looked around the kitchen again, I began to feel everything as a colorful vision floating in space.

"Even these bodies, yours and mine, are appearing inside this *room*."

Mykonos finished his glass. I refilled our glasses. We drank again.

"Most people, they feel stuck in the *room*. They believe they are physical bodies in a physical room, and that is that. You know? Most people spend their entire lives believing that what they see is everything. Until they die. Then it all washes away, and they find themselves in another *room*, bewildered."

We continued to drink.

"Some people get a little spiritual. They have mystical experiences or whatever, and they begin to step outside of the *room*. They realize that they were never in the *room* to begin with, that all the time they thought they were in the *room*, living their little lives, they were actually outside the *room*. All along, they were the space outside the *room*—the deep space of consciousness—but they forgot it, and so they got lost in the goings-on inside the *room*. They got lost in the drama of their little lives and forgot the immensity of who they really are."

Mykonos looked outside the window and paused.

"Those people," he continued, "those *spiritual* people," he said, with more than a hint of sarcasm, "they begin to think the *room* is bad, because it is so brief, so limited. They begin to think that life is bad. And especially, they begin to think that pleasure is bad. Sex is bad. If the *room* changes after death, if it isn't eternal, why bother?"

Mykonos paused to drink sake, and then continued.

"Yes, my friend, most people are stuck inside the *room*, thinking it is all there is, living their lives dedicated to an ever-changing vision that is going to evaporate sooner or later, and so underneath their fake smiles and fragile relationships they are afraid. Or, they are desperately hoping that it is better to get outside the *room* once and for all, doing their best to get ready to leave the *room*, meditating their way into emptiness, praying their way to heaven—or whatever—being 'good' and 'spiritual' so they can leave all of these suffering, sexing bodies behind and get outside the *room* of changes, and rest in eternal peace."

Mykonos drank the rest of the sake in his glass, placed the glass down on the table, turned from the window, and looked directly into my eyes.

"I, however, find it far more interesting," Mykonos said with a smile, "to be both inside the *room* and outside the *room* at the same time."

Mykonos held my gaze longer than usual.

And then I felt it. I was trying to escape the *room* through my spiritual practices, trying to achieve some kind of safety outside the *room*. I was not willing to be vulnerable and fully alive in the *room*, and yet, strangely enough, I was also afraid to let go of everything in the *room* and surrender my entire life—my work, my relationships, my ambitions—dying to the *room*, standing eternally outside the *room*, totally free. I was afraid to stay, and I was afraid to go.

"Drink your sake," Mykonos said, and suddenly I felt the Great One—the same depth I saw in his eyes—alive as everything and everyone. This room, including our two bodies drinking sake, obviously appeared as this free openness, alive as vast love without bounds.

"Yesss. To be outside and inside the *room* at the same time. Why not? Hmmm? Imagine a woman's body with your body, right now, inside the *room*. Why would you want to avoid that? Hmmm?"

"I wouldn't."

"You seem to be inside the *room* drinking with me right now," Mykonos said. "And yet, you can feel the entire *room* and both of us appearing here. You don't have to leave the *room* to be free. Right now, you are already free—outside the *room*, so to speak—witnessing all the comings and goings, *and* appearing as a body, feeling, thinking, wanting to fuck, and so forth, are you not?"

"Yes."

"Can you think of a better way to spend your time inside the *room* than celebrating appearance as love? Dancing with the ladies? Bringing love to this place? Standing outside the *room*, already free, while loving inside the *room*, as a body? Hmmm? Would you rather it be different?"

"No."

"Good, because that's the way it is, my friend. If you forget that you are outside the *room*, you begin to feel trapped by life, so you start looking for a way to be free inside the *room*, but you can't find freedom there. You're stuck inside the *room* with all its inevitable pain and pleasure and death. Even if things seem pretty good right now, you are constantly tense and afraid, because you know things could get bad any time, and in any case, you will die."

Mykonos paused to drink some sake.

"On the other hand, if you get a taste of death, or if you get a little spiritual, then you might prefer to be outside the *room*, standing as the clear space, eternally untouched by all this cycling of pain and pleasure. But to do that, to stand outside of it all, you have to avoid the ladies, you know? Because they'll suck you back into the *room* every time, you know what I mean?"

"Yes."

"Women or God, that's the traditional choice for so-called spiritual men, you see. But it is a completely unnecessary choice. Women are God, sex is God, *everything* is God, and God is beyond everything, too. My advice to you, my friend, is to dance with the ladies, love them completely, but never forget that you are also outside the *room*, right now. That's what women want from you, anyway. They want to feel you inside the *room*, totally with them, and yet absolutely free and unafraid of life. They want to feel you freely awakened outside the *room*, even while you are pressing your flesh-body against theirs. Hmmm?"

"Yeah, I can feel that."

"Good. Just remember, nobody wants to be free. Not really. Nobody is willing to open as love. That's why I'm always on patrol. More sake!"

As I got up to heat more sake, Zelda walked in.

"Hello, my dear," Mykonos said to her, even though they had never met.

"Hi," Zelda responded.

"Mykonos, this is Zelda," I said introducing them. Mykonos looked her up and down. He smiled and nodded his head.

"Yes," Mykonos said, "I can see where *this* night is going. Would you like some sake, my dear?" Mykonos asked Zelda.

"Sure."

After heating the sake, I poured three glasses.

"Let us drink then," Mykonos lifted his glass. "To the Great One."

Zelda and I joined in the toast, and we all drank and talked until Lemuel, Paco, and Layla arrived. Unexpectedly, Dimitri and his girlfriend Michelle also showed up, as did Paco's new girlfriend, Erin. We all moved from the kitchen to the living room, where we listened to music and danced. Eventually, we all sat down on two couches and listened to Mykonos talk.

"Erin," Mykonos said after a few hours of drinking sake, "you are a very beautiful woman. Does Paco love you like he should?"

"What do you mean?" Erin wondered.

"Does Paco lo-o-o-o-o-v-e you?" Mykonos asked.

"Yeah, I think so."

"Paco?" asked Mykonos.

"What?"

"Do you love this woman?"

"Yeah, I guess."

"Mm-hmm. Just as I thought. This is a beautiful woman, Paco."

"I know."

"I think Paco needs some more sake," Mykonos said, laughing.

I began to wonder whether it was a good idea to have my friends get together with Mykonos. Paco, in particular, could be quite moody. Mykonos didn't seem to mind, though. He was laughing and drinking and swaying left and right as he sat on the couch and spoke.

"Paco, can I ask you a question?" Mykonos asked.

"Sure."

"Have you *ever* loved a woman? I mean, really, really loved her?"

"Well, I think I have, but I'm not sure what you mean."

"Then you haven't," Mykonos announced. "I think it is time again to dance."

"Wait a minute. Why are you asking me these questions? Does it feel like I'm not loving Erin?"

Mykonos inhaled with a hiss through his front teeth.

"Paco, my friend, what do you feel, right now, in your heart?"

"I don't know. Not much."

"Your friends here are going to die. *You* are going to die. Erin is going to die."

Erin moved on the couch to be next to Paco. Her eyes were moist. She put her head on Paco's lap, hugging him around his belly.

"This is a fine, fine woman, Paco," Mykonos said. "She wants to feel your heart. We all want to feel your heart."

"Well, maybe I don't want to give you my heart."

"Fuck you, Paco," Mykonos said quietly.

We all sat in silence.

"She has great tits," Dimitri suddenly offered with a sake-fueled smile, gazing at Erin's nipple-puckered shirt.

"Wow! Indeed she does!" Mykonos chimed in, seemingly delighted at Dimitri's sudden outburst.

"Erin, would you like to show Dimitri your breasts?" Mykonos asked.

"Yes, I would," she said, to my surprise. Erin sat up and pulled her shirt off over her head. She wasn't wearing a bra, and her nipples pointed up at a happy angle.

"And you won't give her your heart, Paco," Mykonos said quietly. Then, turning to me, Mykonos shouted, "Why are you still wearing clothes?"

I stood up and took off my clothes, then sat back down on the couch.

"Jesus, you're hairy," Mykonos said, looking at my legs.

"Mykonos, why are *you* still wearing clothes?" Layla challenged.

"Because nobody has taken them off of me yet!"

Layla immediately pulled off Mykonos's tank top and shorts, then took off her own clothes. Lemuel, Zelda, Dimitri, and Michelle followed. Only Paco remained fully clothed.

"Are we all happy to be together?" Mykonos asked.

"Yes," everybody answered.

"Is there anybody here who is afraid of pleasure?"

"Not me," Layla answered, teasingly stroking Mykonos's belly. We were all quite drunk.

"Oh, really?" Mykonos raised an eyebrow at Layla. "How much pleasure have you ever experienced in that chubby little body of yours?"

Layla laughed. Then she spread her legs and began to rub the inside of her thighs as she sat on the couch next to Mykonos. She slid down so her butt was almost off the cushion, caressing her skin, licking her lips.

"Yesss. These bodies are capable of great pleasure—and pain—during their brief span. Show it to me, ma. Show me your pleasure."

Layla was really getting into touching herself. Her eyes were closed and she began to moan. She began thrusting against her own hands.

Paco got up and left the room.

"Yesss. Now, Layla my dear, can you take the pleasure from your cunt and let it spread into your heart? Hmmm? Can you open your heart as big as your pussy is open? Breathe that fuck all the way into your heart. Feel your whole body and heart as one big cunt. Wide open. Hmmm? Show us the pleasure of your love, ma, filling your whole body!"

Layla was moving on fire with pleasure, her chest and face flush red. She mouthed words of ecstasy, silently repeating "cunt" and "fuck" as she touched herself with more and more abandon.

I could hear Paco in the kitchen, opening and closing cupboards. Everyone else was watching Layla pleasure herself.

"Open your eyes, Layla. Look at Zelda," Mykonos said. "Show her your body wide open. Show her your pleasure. Let us all see your body fucked open by God alive as love!"

Layla opened her eyes and continued touching herself. She looked into Zelda's eyes, and Zelda smiled, shyly. Layla began looking at all of us as she touched herself, her mouth opening and closing. "Cunt," she said quietly, humping her hand.

"Yesss. Cunt. A cunt as big as love," Mykonos said, looking at Layla. "Paco!" Mykonos shouted, still looking at Layla. "What the hell are you doing in there?"

"Looking for something to eat," Paco yelled from the kitchen.

"Have you ever seen a woman open her whole body as love, Paco?" Mykonos shouted. "Layla is opening as big as the universe! Paco, a woman is showing her heart and shining her cunt as God's light in here!"

"I'm busy," came Paco's voice from the kitchen.

Zelda sat down next to Layla and started stroking her, then gently kissing her neck and breasts.

"Women are beautiful, are they not?" Mykonos asked.

"Yes they are!" Dimitri answered, almost jumping out of his chair.

"Women are definitely beautiful," Lemuel agreed.

"I love women!" Dimitri's girlfriend, Michelle, answered.

We suddenly realized that Erin was no longer in the room. I got up and looked through the house for Erin, checking the bathroom, the bedrooms, and finally the kitchen, where I found her and Paco sitting at the table, talking.

"I don't know what you want," Paco said to Erin.

"I just want you, Paco."

"You have me."

"I wish I did."

"What's up?" I asked.

"We're having a personal discussion. We'd rather be alone right now," Paco answered.

Erin stared down at the top of the kitchen table. I saw Paco's temples bulge as he ground his jaw.

"Ok. I'll check in with you later," I said, and went back to join the others.

Layla's eyes were closed as she ran her hands from her knees up the inside of her thighs and back down. Zelda was touching Layla, kissing Layla's breasts. Michele and Dimitri were making out as they danced slowly. Lemuel was drinking sake and smiling.

When I sat down, Mykonos began speaking to me.

"Here we are. It's a beautiful evening. We are dancing, enjoying being alive as bodies. It's warm and the air is moist. But we could be in the desert." Mykonos looked at me intensely. "Imagine it's so dry that your throat is parched. The harsh desert wind is blowing. We are alone. There are no people, plants, or animals for as far as you can see. Can you feel that as the *room* we are in, right now?"

I could feel it. Mykonos had a way of painting the most vivid visions with his words.

"Or maybe we are in the late 1800's," Mykonos continued. "Right now, we are in the midst of a battlefield. Dead bodies lay on the ground around us. Someone is coming at you with a knife. Hmmm? Feel that completely."

Mykonos was changing channels on our minds' TV screen, and the show changed in the *room*. We were in the show—in the desert, or on the battlefield—and also watching the show as it changed from scene to scene.

"When you die, you get sucked back into any *room* that you need. Time only is fixed inside each *room*. From outside the *room*, the 1800's didn't happen before the 1900's. Every place, every time, is happening now, and you can reincarnate into any place, into more than one place and time, whatever you need, whatever you hold onto. Look around the *room* you are in right now."

I looked at Dimitri kissing Michelle deeply, their tongues darting into each other's mouth while they swayed together nakedly. I saw Zelda and Layla laughing and touching. Lemuel was watching everyone as he drank. Mykonos began stroking his own penis.

"Most people never grow beyond their teenage mind, wanting to be sexually desired, wanting to be sexually loved. This *room*, this human realm that we find ourselves in, is about sex, primarily. After you die, if you are still fascinated, still attracted by sex—ZAP!—this is the place you come to see. This is the *room* you inhabit. You could be in any *room*. Even now, with a little bit of practice, you can occupy any *room*. You can meditate and enter a *room* of gliding lights, where everything is pastel and gold. You can meditate on an empty *room*, where no thing is. People do that, you know. They meditate for years and go into other *rooms*, other realms, other places."

Mykonos looked at his empty sake glass, and I filled it for him. He drank, looked around, and continued to stroke his erection.

"You see, there are all kinds of places you can find yourself, *will* find yourself. And yet, they are all just *rooms*. Some are ugly, horrible places, and others are very pleasurable. Like dreams at night, you will drift in and out of all kinds of *rooms*, in your life and after death. Most people haven't the slightest idea that they are in a *room* right now. They go about their lives as if it were all leading somewhere magnificent. They don't know that it's just one scene after another, all equally—eerily—dissatisfying. Other people get a glimpse. They see that they are in a *room*, and they realize that they can change *rooms*. So they do whatever they have to in order to leave this *room* and get to a better place—meditate, take drugs, pray that when they die they will go to a different *room*, a more heavenly place."

Mykonos looked at my crotch and looked away. I knew he was suggesting that I stroke myself like he was doing. It felt a bit odd, but I began to masturbate.

"It all looks quite different when you are inside the *room* and outside the *room* at the same time, does it not? Here we are, in a room with naked women, lovers dancing, a little drunk, even *erect*," Mykonos said, motioning his head toward my crotch. "And at the same time, you can feel the *room*. Yes? You can feel this all appearing. Time itself, appearing in place. What a wonder, hmmm? Standing free, outside of the *room* as the scenes come and go, and yet totally in the *room*, you know? In the *room* with a hard cock, you know what I mean? Not afraid. Not partially in the *room*, because you know it is all suffering, because you want out. But *entirely* in the *room*. So *in* the *room*, you *are* the entire *room*! You are the walls, the floor, you are every body, and you are your hard cock! All of it is appearing, and you are not afraid to be any of it!"

Shivers ran up my spine as Mykonos spoke. I could feel the whole *room* as me, and all of it shimmering as a dream or a movie filled with characters. But I wasn't just standing outside of it, watching it. I *was* it.

"You see what sex is then, don't you? To have no need, no holding, no craven obsession. And yet to be erect, fucking everything open as love, bringing light into this *room*, into this place, into your woman and friends, fearlessly, with no need for victory, with no sense of defeat. Alive as light down to your cock! The war is already won, love-bliss is already the substance of every place that appears and every part of you, and yet the holy war appears to continue in every *room*, so I remain on patrol. I don't know. Maybe I'm mad."

Mykonos took another drink, looked around the room, and then he looked right at me.

"You have nothing to fear. You are already dead. This is the other side," Mykonos smiled while he stroked himself.

"Why is it exactly this way?" Mykonos asked, not waiting for an answer. "I don't know. I can't account for it myself. It is a vast mystery of love, not other than you, hmmm?"

Mykonos sat back and looked around the room. He shook his head and smiled.

"Look at Layla touching herself. Lost in the *room* of her own sensation. And Dimitri, dancing with his bride. Recognized as the Great One, everything is obviously alive as love. Yet every thing and every body turns to shit. Every body here will be buried in the ground in a few years. If anyone really felt where their little life was going, they would kill themselves in despair, pleasure themselves to death, or go insane—or realize that they are not stuck in the *room* they are seeing. But they don't have to go to another *room*, either, like some goddamn religious zealot. Already, right now, even as this *room* appears, even as any *room* appears, now, during dreams, after death—and we don't really know what this *room* is right now, do we? It could be a vision occurring after our last death, hmmm? It could even be a very real dream we have yet to awaken from—but in any case, right now, you are feeling itself, the deep space of consciousness in which the *room* appears, whatever the *room* is. You are already free, open, unlimited—you don't need to know anything else, or experience one more moment of this or any *room*. Do you have any idea what I'm talking about, mutant?"

"Yes," I answered.

"Yes, you do. But look at Dimitri over there. He's not even in the same *room*, you know what I mean? This isn't a secret teaching. It is self-secret, you know? It may seem like we are all in the same *room*, but look around you. Nobody else can even hear me."

Zelda and Layla were totally absorbed in their own play, and Lemuel had now joined them, rubbing their naked bodies with his hands. Dimitri and Michelle were dancing, kissing, holding onto each other like newlyweds.

"Keep stroking your cock, you hairy bastard," Mykonos said to me. "As you do, look around. Feel the *room*. Breathe it in, the entire appearance. It's a living vision. It is *she*. Don't run from her. Don't try to find safety. There isn't any. You are either alive as fuck, fully in her even while you stand free, or you are lost in her and feel trapped. And she's gonna do a number on your body in any case. Your body is her food. She's gonna eat you, as all things are eaten and made into other things. Can you feel—as you are—outside of this *room*, even while you stay hard?"

"Yes, I'm able to do that right now."

"Good. Because this is all there is. God. The He and the She of it. And She always comes in two. There always seems like there is a choice. You know, better and worse. Good and bad. Pleasure and pain. But if you believe that, she's got you. There is no choice, no real choice, because she appears as she does, and you are the place of her appearance, you know? You are already free even as she dances, right now. The point isn't to get away from her, my friend. The point is, to *be* her. Not as a practice, but as simple love-recognition, because you *are* her. Just relax, feel every part of her, breathe her, love her—love *as* her, with your whole body, including your pecker, no matter how she shows herself to you."

Suddenly, the whole scene seemed like a seedy sex party. The women weren't that attractive to me. Zelda's breasts seemed lifeless. Layla was acting obnoxious. Dimitri and Michelle were in a world of their own. Lemuel seemed very drunk and lost in the novelty of so much naked flesh. Paco and Erin were arguing in the kitchen. It had seemed interesting, but now the whole gathering seemed boring.

And yet, as Mykonos spoke, everything came alive as a vision. The whole scene, the entire appearing world, was *she*, as Mykonos said, showing herself. Mykonos's voice was reminding me over and over of the who, the what, and the where of every scene, of the whole appearance. Even the furniture and the air felt alive as conscious light appearing as love's openness.

I wasn't just witnessing the *room*, I was alive as the show itself, recognizing the Great One opening as forms of love. I wasn't just standing outside of the *room*, I was fully *in* the *room*, open *as* the *room*, with a hard cock.

"Yes," Mykonos said, "God is Fuck. I have told you this before. Why be afraid of incarnation? You are appearing as a body in this *room* while also standing as free consciousness outside this *room*. Let go of everything. Be willing to let everything appear and disappear as love. Hmmm? Are you *that* free? Are you willing to stand wide open, alive as everything that comes and goes, even if nothing appears at all? Stand open, now, playing the whole *room* and your entire body open as love, full as love, down to your pecker, down to your toes! Receive the love-force of God down into your head, down into your heart, down into your cock, your feet. Open and let love's force press down into you, like thick water filling you, pressing down into this *room*. Be alive as love without limit. Hmmm? Would you rather contract your heart and body and struggle with women, work, and seeming complication? Do you want to be an asshole, like Paco?" Mykonos asked me.

Just then, I saw Paco entering the living room, his shoulders hunched like a beaten man.

"What's up, Paco?" I asked.

"Just the usual shit."

"Paco, is your cock hard?" Mykonos asked him.

"What?"

"Do you have an e-r-e-c-t-i-o-n?" Mykonos asked, sounding out "erection" as if it were a careful pronunciation of a word from a foreign language.

"What are you talking about?" Paco asked, as he noticed we were stroking our cocks.

"My friend," Mykonos said, "sit down and have some sake with us."

I poured the last of the sake, and we all drank. Paco mostly stared at the floor.

"What's wrong with this picture?" Mykonos asked Paco.

Paco remained silent.

"Paco, do you enjoy wearing clothes while everybody else dances naked, showing their flesh to the world, ecstatic and free as love's body?"

"I don't care."

"Paco, look at your friends here."

Paco looked around the room. He looked at Mykonos and I stroking our genitals, and he shook his head in disgust.

"Do you masturbate, Paco?" Mykonos asked.

"Sometimes."

"Well, are you ashamed of it?"

"I'm not ashamed of it, but I wouldn't do it in public."

"This isn't public, Paco. We're among friends."

"Well, I wouldn't do it among friends."

"Why not?" Mykonos asked.

"Because it's a private thing."

"Yes, for most people it is, Paco. They hide in their rooms to indulge in secret pleasures while their lives pass in unspoken suffering. But here, among friends, among loved ones, why not share your joy? Why not show your pleasure? Hmmm? Why would you want to hide your body's pleasure?"

Paco didn't answer.

"And if you aren't afraid to show your pleasure, Paco, if you aren't afraid to *feel* pleasure in your entire body without shame, without fear, without guilt, then maybe you can even open your heart a little bit and shine your love a little bit to all. Your cock is hanging from your heart, you know. Yank that thing while you breathe love down into your heart, into your whole body. Yank your pecker while you open yourself to God, Paco. Be invaded by the force of love pressing down into you and let it open your heart, fill your belly, and enliven your genitals. When your head is relaxed open so love can press down into you, when you can take it deep into your heart like a cunt pressed open by God's fuck, then you can *be* love, *show* love, and *give* love without fear. Otherwise, what is sex but a little trickle of energy through the nervous system, a spastic release of middle-class tension?"

"But I'm not sexually turned on right now," Paco explained.

"Of course not. Your chest is caved in. Your belly is tense. Your jaw is clenched. How can love enter you when your whole body is tight as a fist? Dance, Paco. Get up and dance. Open your body and breathe. Feel the Great One right now, moving through and opening these ugly bodies of dying flesh. They're just bodies, Paco. They have a few years left in them, maybe, but they are just meat-bodies—unless you relax and feel the Great One living you, unless you consent and breathe the Great One deep into your heart, deep into your belly and cock. Then your body can open and be a living force of love in the world. And with your woman, Paco. That's all she really wants from you. You can talk with her forever—until you can fuck her open to God and breathe her open in love's bliss, she's going to give you her boo-hoo and long face."

Mykonos stood up and began dancing, if that's what you would call it. His feet remained planted on the ground as he raised his hands in the air, pulling back his lips so his front teeth showed, and he bobbed up and down, left and right. Mykonos was one of the worst dancers I have ever seen, and yet his dancing made me smile and open my heart. Dimitri turned up the music. I stopped masturbating and sat back on the couch, relaxing, breathing, and opening as Mykonos had instructed.

Mykonos looked over and saw that Layla had started to pump Lemuel's penis with her hand.

"If you come, Lemuel, make sure you tell us all!" Mykonos shouted above the music as he danced.

Lemuel laid back and smiled. Zelda massaged Lemuel's head and neck as Layla stroked his penis.

From the kitchen, Erin walked into the room, looked around, took off her clothes, and sat down on the couch next to me. Then she laid down and put her head on my naked lap. I wanted to touch her breasts, but Paco was sitting only a few feet away on the other couch, and I knew he was feeling bad. So, I just sat there and watched everyone dance and touch each other.

A knock on the door broke the flow.

Mykonos looked at me, and I was about to get up when I heard the door open and somebody walk in.

It was Adrienne. She was an acquaintance, a friend of the landlord. I had met Adrienne once or twice, but I hardly knew her. She walked into the living room and looked around.

"Looks like I walked into a party," she said.

I was surprised at how nonchalant she seemed. She sat down on a chair near to where Layla was still masturbating Lemuel.

"Are you enjoying the evening, my dear?" Mykonos asked Adrienne while he continued to dance. As far as I knew, Mykonos had never met Adrienne before and didn't know who she was or why she was there.

"Well, I think my evening is about to get better!" Adrienne answered.

"Paco, since you are the only one without someone to dance with at the moment, why don't you dance with this beautiful woman. What is your name?" Mykonos asked.

"Adrienne."

"Paco, it is up to you to welcome Adrienne to our little party."

Paco reluctantly got up, took Adrienne's hand, and they began dancing together, fully clothed.

"Adrienne. You have very large breasts," Mykonos spoke loudly from across the room.

Adrienne smiled at Mykonos. I couldn't believe what he said. Adrienne didn't seem to mind.

"How would you like to take off your shirt and show us your breasts?" Mykonos asked.

"No, thank you. I'm all right as I am," Adrienne answered.

"Yes, you are, my dear," Mykonos responded, and danced his way over to Dimitri and Michelle, who where making out in the corner.

Erin took my hand and moved it to her belly. She obviously wanted me to touch her, but I still felt bad for Paco. I stroked her hair with my other hand. She began crying, quietly.

Erin's naked body, her head in my lap, her vulnerable tears—I wanted to love her and touch her with my whole body. I had been in monogamous relationships all of my life. For more than ten years, I had been faithful to Gia, who I considered my life-partner. I had never had a one-night stand or an affair. In that moment, though, with a crying, naked woman lying on the couch with me, her blonde hair against my thighs, tears running down her face, I could feel that I wanted to touch her.

I hadn't seen Gia for a few weeks. She was supposed to be flying home from a vacation that day, and she might walk in any time. Erin put her hand on top of my hand, which was still on her belly. Her fine, light brown pubic hairs were inches from my fingers. She turned her face toward me and pressed her crying eyes into my belly. Her lips were soft against my belly's skin.

"Inside the *room* and outside the *room* at the same time!" Mykonos shouted as he danced.

Paco seemed to be loosening up while dancing with Adrienne.

"Oh, yuck!" Layla yelled.

Lemuel had ejaculated all over her hand.

"Lemuel, you were supposed to tell us when you were coming!" Mykonos chided.

"I didn't know I was going to come! It just kind of happened."

"Was it pleasurable?" Mykonos asked.

"Yeah. It felt great."

"We wanted to share in your pleasure, Lemuel. We wanted to feel it with you. Next time, let us know. Shout it out. 'I'm coming! I'm coming!'"

"Ok. I'll try!" Lemuel agreed.

"What's wrong, Layla?" Mykonos asked. "You have some kind of biological problem with a man's come?"

"It just surprised me. And now I'm all sticky and gooey. What should I do with it?"

"Whatever you want!" Mykonos said.

Layla went to the kitchen. Lemuel lay back with a relaxed smile on his face. Zelda got up and started dancing with Mykonos, Michelle, and Dimitri.

Hesitantly, I began to move my hand up and down Erin's body, from her belly, down her thighs, to her knees, and back. She was kissing my belly below my navel.

I looked up and saw Michelle and Zelda dancing with Mykonos. Dimitri was now dancing by himself. Michelle began touching Mykonos between his legs. Zelda moved to hug Mykonos from behind, so he was sandwiched between the two women. Zelda reached around to rub his chest from behind and Michelle was holding his genitals in front. Dimitri watched, his dancing becoming less enthusiastic. Finally, Dimitri sat down on the couch, looking despondent.

Mykonos continued to dance. He didn't seem to mind the women touching him, but he also didn't seem to care that much. Michelle's dancing and touching was becoming more and more sexual, more animalistic and savage. She began pulling on Mykonos's balls.

Mykonos continued to dance. Suddenly, Lemuel jumped up and ran to the bathroom.

"Could you check on Lemuel?" Mykonos asked me.

I went to the bathroom and found Lemuel curled around the toilet on the floor. Vomit filled the toilet and ran down its sides. Lemuel smiled weakly through barely opened eyes.

"I guess I drank too much."

"Yeah. I'll bring you a glass of water."

I brought some water to Lemuel and told Mykonos what had happened.

"Ah, yesss. So Lemuel decided to visit Shaker Heights," Mykonos responded. He was referring to an Ohio city near to where both Lemuel and I were born and raised. We grew up together as best friends.

"He's got to learn to breathe it down," Mykonos said about Lemuel. "You see, he can't circulate his pleasure. He lost his spunk on Layla's hand, and now he's bringing it all back home to Shaker Heights."

I didn't know why Mykonos was referring to Lemuel's vomiting as going to Shaker Heights, but somehow it made sense.

"If you're going to sex and drink and open, you've got to know how to breathe the force through you. Spirit—that's what they call alcohol, you know—spirit has a force to it, and if you don't circulate it through you, then it has to come out somewhere, hmmm? Most people can only take so much pleasure, so much life force and openness, before they pop, one way or the other. Your friend has got to learn to breathe it through him, down the front and up the back, or else he's going to be spending his life visiting Shaker Heights. He's got to grow and learn to love without breaking the circle of life in his body. Life isn't about stimulating yourself until you spasm, throwing off life's energy through your dick or your mouth or your mind. Life is about opening as love, way bigger than the body, as the whole *room*, the whole damn circle, from the highest to the lowest and everything in between, you know what I mean?"

"Aaaiiiii!" Michelle screamed. She writhed and danced like a madwoman, kneeling and taking Mykonos into her mouth.

"Do you like cock?" Mykonos asked her.

She nodded yes as she looked up into his eyes.

"Have you always liked cock?"

She nodded again.

"Yesss. Michelle worships cock. It's not this cock or that cock. It's cock. Michelle is a cock worshipper. Look at her open and take it down."

Michelle was gone. She sucked and groaned, drool coming down her chin and neck. Her eyes were rolling, opening and closing. She couldn't get enough. Zelda released Mykonos and started dancing, watching Michelle swallow Mykonos like a madwoman.

"Layla enjoys being with a man and getting him off," Mykonos said, "But look at Michelle. She worships cock. Hmmm? It's a different thing."

Layla walked in from the kitchen and asked, "Why is Lemuel laying on the floor in the bathroom?"

"He puked," I answered.

Layla sat down next to Dimitri and watched Michelle suck Mykonos.

Dimitri immediately got up and left the room. I wasn't sure if he walked into another room or if he left the house.

"Some women are wives," Mykonos said, as he sat down on the couch. Michelle crawled on her knees to where Mykonos was sitting and resumed taking him in her mouth, ferociously. She didn't seem to notice we were all watching. Mykonos smiled, shook his head, and continued.

"You see, some women want to find a good man to love. Cock to a woman like this is always part of her man, the man who she loves, the man who she opens to God with. Other women—women like Michelle—are cock worshipers. It's a whole 'nother thing. They want to open and take cock. It's their way of opening to the Great One, of surrendering open and taking the Great One so deep they are lost in the worship, gone in the giving of themselves, gone in their love of cock—not of a man as a character, as a husband or boyfriend, but gone in the love of cock itself. Wifely women can't fake that they are into cock—they may be into their man's cock, but not any cock. Women like Michelle, on the other hand, they can certainly love a man, but they will always worship cock. No woman should be forced to be something she is not."

Mykonos started talking to Michelle, who was still ravenously mouthing him. "Yesss. Open all the way. Take it down into your heart, ma. Open so wide you feel the Great One bursting open your whole body to infinity. Take it and open like you've always wanted to."

The room filled with intense energy. This was more than oral sex. It felt more like a religious vision. The air felt thick, as if a heavy pleasure were pressing down into our bodies. My point of view changed, so I felt as if I was outside the *room*, as Mykonos had spoken, feeling the entire room and everyone in it, an arising vision of thick color, heavy with love-bliss, and yet I was also in the *room*, as a body. Tears were streaming down Michelle's face in adoration of cock. She was fully abandoned in her passionate ministrations, in rapture, as were we all.

Erin began to breath more quickly, and her tears of sadness changed to bliss. She sat up from my lap and began laughing. Her hands lifted over her head. Her arms extended upward and her fingers spread, filled by the ecstasy pressing us all open. Her legs began to tremble and her mouth opened. Her head tilted back, her throat stretched open, and her fingers splayed with the pressure of love's force.

Even Paco seemed filled with love's pressure. His arms extended to his sides and his palms opened wide. His breath became deeper, and he began weeping.

Layla leaned forward to get a closer look at the cock worship. Her face seemed a bit tense, perhaps jealous.

My entire body felt filled with a force, the same force of thick love that filled the room, that was the *room*. My breath deepened and my belly grew large, filled with the love-substance that was the *room*. My limbs felt like they were filling with force, my whole body alive and open.

And yet I also felt entirely unaffected. Nothing. Vast space, more *nothing* than space, full as this appearing *room*, thick as love, yet untouched, unrippled by its appearance. My body and mind were blown open by love, and yet something was as it always was, unchanged, unmoved.

"This reminds me of parties I went to in the '60's," Adrienne said.

"My dear," Mykonos said to Adrienne while Michelle continued between his legs, "the 60's were about liberation from social constraints—this is about liberation *from* everything *as* everything. Can you open your heart and body so much there is no more open to go? Hmmm? Are you willing to offer your love—in your way, not necessarily like Michelle here—so that you disappear in the giving of yourself and yet are alive as everything? Are you willing to offer yourself as if to a lover—offering your breath, your body, your mind, every part of you—wide open, so you are invaded by the Great One, fucked open by the Great One, simply alive as the love that you are, alive as all, lived by the Great One appearing as this place, all these bodies, space itself?"

"I'm not so sure about that," Adrienne answered.

"Well, that's why this feels like it does to you. Unless you are willing to be *possessed* by love, you are just a woman with very large breasts who happens to be enjoying herself with some very strange people."

"I am enjoying myself, quite a bit, really. You all are great."

Paco hugged Erin.

"That's right, Paco," Mykonos said. "Let your heart break."

Paco was crying so hard he began convulsing as he held Erin in his arms.

Lemuel walked in from the bathroom, smiling, his hair messed and his eyes bloodshot. "What have I missed?" he asked.

Nobody answered.

3
Thimble

༄

The next day, I slept until the afternoon. The night had been long. Gia had arrived home late—her plane had been delayed—and she joined us all dancing, weeping in ecstasy, and listening to Mykonos. The house was filled with a tangible air of bliss and openness, and Gia fit right in. At some point near dawn, people went home or retired to various rooms in the house.

Layla ended up going to sleep in a room with Mykonos. Paco and Erin slept in another room. Dimitri never came back that evening, and Michelle went home by herself, as did Adrienne. Gia and I went to bed, only to have Zelda knock on our bedroom door as we were falling asleep.

"What's going on?" I asked Zelda.

"I thought I heard someone in the bushes outside the house."

I went outside and walked around the house, checking all the bushes, and found nothing.

Zelda sat on our bed, her head hanging low.

"If you want, you can spend the night with us," I told her.

Gia agreed, and Zelda seemed happy.

We turned off the light and all got into the same bed. Gia and I had never shared a bed with another woman before.

Before long, perhaps still stimulated from the evening events and the sake, Gia began kissing me and fondling my penis. I was very conscious of Zelda lying next to us. Gia ducked under the covers and began sucking me. I turned to look at Zelda. She was gazing right into my eyes.

Gia pulled down the covers to completely expose my body, and continued moving her mouth on my cock. She reached out her hand and began to touch Zelda, taking Zelda's hand and putting it on me. Zelda moved closer to us, grabbing me firmly with her hand and holding the base of my penis as Gia continued mouthing me.

I found this to be incredibly erotic. Gia inviting another woman to touch me. I lay back and enjoyed a long-time fantasy.

And then a strange thing happened. The erotic sensation felt less than open. I was grinding my mind into feeling how great it was, tensing my body as I approached an orgasm. This was the kind of fantasy that I had always wanted to live out, and yet it felt bad, like eating a gourmet dish that I knew should taste good but didn't. Compared to how open the whole evening felt, our threesome felt relatively closed, paltry, superficial.

I remembered Mykonos's instruction, and I relaxed. I felt this scene—Gia giving me head while Zelda held my cock—arising in the *room*. I felt through and beyond my own body's sensations and the appearance of the scene, opening as the space in which the *room* was arising. I relaxed open and felt the entire moment rippling as a mirage in this space that was boundless and free, the space that I relaxed open as. At the same time, I was incredibly turned on by the two women on my cock.

My breath opened, my body relaxed, my belly filled with a force of love that that was the substance of the whole *room*. I no longer felt centered in my body, but was open as everything, including Gia and Zelda. Each of their bodies felt as much me as my body did. Their bodies, my body, the bed, the wall, the sounds, even the space between us, shone as open heart-feeling. No separation tensed the obvious openness of being.

Gia began to rub my swelling belly as she sucked. Zelda looked into my eyes, and her eyes moistened. I felt our bodies' move as art, an appearance of love, magnifying love through their care and fondle, opening as the love that was alive as the entire moment, the substance of the *room* and everything in it.

Fountains of light shot up my spine exploding as colors above. Feeling open as the whole room, the rain of color descended through us all, through the air, thick bliss, and Gia and Zelda moaned and wept and shuddered, and loved. No boundaries shored the flow, so even time liquefied as space, suspending sex's thrill as open awe. Touching each other, looking into each other's eyes, we knew love without limit. Certainty exploded as our bodies' appearance, vanishing, appearing, loving.

A soft eternity, evanescent and bare, exposed all showing as love's bliss. Our play eased open as a motionless peal of light, heart-infinite, undoubtable, complete, gone to God.

Eventually, we slept. When I woke in the afternoon, Zelda and Gia were gone.

I called Mykonos on the phone just to check in.

"Have you seen Adrienne today?" he asked me.

"No."

"Do you have her phone number?"

"Yes, why?" I wondered, since Mykonos never called anyone.

"I just want to smooth anything out that needed smoothing out."

Mykonos ended up spending the afternoon with Adrienne. Then he came over to my house, and told me about it.

"She's doing fine," he said. "It's always important to keep your friends close, but your enemies closer."

Mykonos held my gaze for just a moment longer than necessary, to make sure I understood the point he was making.

"Zelda came by and visited me earlier today," Mykonos told me.

"Really?"

"Mm-hmm. Did you fuck her last night?" he asked me.

"No."

"She was glowing. She was radiant with fuck. Are you sure you didn't fuck her?"

"Yes, I'm sure." I described to Mykonos what had happened with Gia, Zelda, and me.

"Sex. It means so much to people. For some people, it's the only way they really let themselves open to God. Zelda's one of them. She could have the vision of God thrust in her face day after day, but an hour of fuck—even feeling Gia sucking on your pecker—and she's transformed."

Mykonos went on to describe the different types of men and women, and how they relate to sex and God.

"People spend most of their lives wanting more sex, better sex, deeper sex. Sex is probably the main reason that people don't really open to God—typical sex, that is. The Great One is always present, alive as everything, as everyone. But people are contracting into sexual hope, into their ideas about sex, wanting more romance, more emotional connection, more passion. Most people never fuck in their lives. Not really. You know what I mean?"

"Yes."

"Most men are satisfied with a quick squirt. And most women are fine with feeling loved, feeling adored. Women want to be adored by a man, and men want their dicks treated like they were God, you know? But unless you open to the Great One, sex is nothing but bondage."

Mykonos paused.

"Do you have a cigarette?"

I went to the closet and got Mykonos a cigarette from the stash I kept for him.

Mykonos lit up and took a drag. He looked out of the window as we sat in the kitchen. I waited for him to continue speaking.

"This place is about fuck," he said. "This human realm, we are all fighting for something, but for most people it's about sex. You know what I mean by sex, don't you? The whole damn thing. It's not just pussy and cock. It's homes and children and security and comfort. It's jealousy and loneliness and hope. It's time itself. Everyone wants to get laid. *Really* laid. Some seek it through making money, or having a family, or achieving power or fame. But it's fuck they want. Fuck. To be smithereened in bliss, opened beyond all limits, loved absolutely, to give themselves completely—to infinity. Fuck."

He took a long drag from his cigarette, and exhaled slowly.

"How long do you think Zelda will be radiant with fuck? Hmmm? I know what happened here last night," he said, looking deeply into my eyes, before looking out the window again and pausing to smoke. "You laid the dharma on her heart. You fucked her open, even though you didn't actually put your pecker in her, you know?"

"Yes."

"But poor Zelda, she's going to beam for a day or two, and then it's going to fade. She'll be moping again, boo-hooing because she doesn't have a boyfriend, looking at her fatty wagon in the mirror and watching herself get old."

I could feel Zelda's life so clearly as Mykonos spoke.

"You know, my friend, what happened last night with all of us, I don't know why it happened. It just happened. That kind of thing can't be planned. We all came together—each in our own way—and the evening came and went. It was something. And it was nothing. You know what I mean? Talking too much about something like that ruins its magic. We all felt what we did. But some of us will be able to continue opening, and some of us won't."

"I know what you mean," I said, thinking of Zelda. And Paco. And Dimitri.

"An ocean can fall on your head," Mykonos said looking at me, "but if all you have is a thimble, then you can only catch so much."

Mykonos gazed into the distance. He held his cigarette between his lips and began rhythmically clapping the base of his palms together.

"When you fuck a woman," he said, putting his cigarette down on the edge of the table, "you want to breathe the light down and fill her. It's a rhythmic thing," he said, clapping his hands together again, "the pulse of the universe. Bam, bam, bam, radiating out from the center, nobody in the way, the Great One radiating out as fuck, shining as all things, alive as love. Women know this, intuitively. Women know in their bodies that God is fuck, but few get the chance to really open, you know. So they settle for babies and a nice house."

Mykonos stopped clapping and looked at me. "There's nothing wrong with babies and a nice house, of course."

"I know what you're talking about, Mykonos."

"It's just that every woman is the universe. Every woman is She, and so she waits for He, and he never quite gets there." Mykonos started clapping again. "He never quite makes it to that second notch, where fuck becomes more than sex, where it becomes the pulse of God, and the woman knows who she is because the man knows who she is and fucks her *as* she is. Breathe the Great One down into you and fuck her open as you both open without end," his hands still clapping together, "hitting that second notch over and over, which isn't a physical place in her pussy so much as it is the place in her heart that is unseparate from you, hmmm?"

I nodded.

"And here she is, all around you, now," Mykonos said, looking around the room. "You can fuck this moment open just like you would fuck a woman, feeling into her, loving her, opening her as the space beyond the *room* here, who you are, who she is, even as your bodies fuck," Mykonos clapped his hands together, "or as you breathe, even now." Mykonos clapped his hands together with our breaths.

"Breathing her, fucking her, loving her, in any case you *are* her. And until you open as her, and beyond her, she will complain."

Mykonos smiled, and asked for another cigarette. After lighting it, he took a few long drags, and continued.

"A woman's energy sometimes seems chaotic, but she is only waiting to be known, recognized for who she is. She intuits that your recognition of her is somehow necessary for her recognition of herself. Do you know what I'm saying?"

"Yes, I think so."

"She needs to be seen to know herself, because she is light, she is all, and when she is seen fully, when you really see her as she is, then she dies in bliss." Mykonos laughed. He began to sing, totally off key, "Killing me softly with his words, killing me softly, with his words, telling my whole life, with his words, killing me softly…" Mykonos stopped singing and began clapping his hands together. "To love her fully is to open her to death, and that's when she knows who she is, who you are, what is, altogether."

"When you can reach that second notch," Mykonos continued, bam, bam, clapping the base of his palms together, "then you can fuck her to death, you fuck her to God, beyond knowablity, alive as all, transparent as light, taken by the Great One, you know? Even now."

My skin felt like it dissolved, so that my body had no bounds. Edges seemed vanished as openness. Mykonos sat still and quiet. A force shot down opening my belly large as my breath deepened. A clear light seemed to fill the room so even objects seemed translucent. And at depth nothing changed at all. Mykonos had once again revealed the source or place of this *room*, as all, behind all, alive as all.

"Why don't you call your friends and let's have some lunch," Mykonos suggested.

4
Blue Truth

∽

At Mykonos's suggestion, I telephoned Lemuel, Paco, and Dimitri, inviting them to lunch. We all met at an outdoor café on the beach.

A busboy brought some appetizers, and Mykonos nodded toward the stage where a band was supposed to play later in the afternoon. From a door near the stage the waitress came and made her way toward our table. She was gorgeous. Her hips were wrapped in a purple sarong. Her breasts were held by a small yellow bikini top. Her athletic belly was golden-brown from hot hours in the sun. In the long braid of her blond hair were two bright hibiscus flowers, one yellow, one red.

"Yes," Mykonos said languidly, hissing the final "s" as he usually did when talking about women or God. "Yesss. She is beautiful, is she not?"

We all nodded, in our own way. Lemuel gave his usual slack-jawed, "Uh-huh." Dimitri—who told us he had gone home the previous night when he felt hurt by Michelle's affections toward Mykonos—was more interested in the fish tacos on his plate than the waitress, though he looked up and exclaimed an enthusiastic, "Oh yeah!"

Paco, however, definitely seemed to be in some kind of mood. He stood up from our table, shaking his head and mumbling something to himself, and went to play some beach volleyball not far from where we were sitting.

I couldn't keep my eyes off of the waitress. She seemed perfect. Absolutely beautiful. I wanted her.

"Breathe her in, my friend," Mykonos said softly, "She is all around you."

My attention snapped from the waitress as if from a dream. *She is all around you.* Mykonos had a way of waking me up.

"Mm-hmm. You like her, don't you?" Mykonos asked me.

"Yes."

"You want her."

"Yes."

"Look around. So does everybody else."

I looked around. There were red-faced tourists talking about the scenery and chewing their food. Paco was playing volleyball with a group of young locals on the beach. A few couples sat at tables around us, holding hands, sipping their drinks from huge ice-filled glasses and speaking to each other in voices of quiet affection.

Nobody seemed to notice the waitress, who had stopped at the table right next to ours to take an order. She was in her early twenties, probably a college student or a surfer who was making some extra money for the summer, waitressing at this beachside café and bar. Her skin was flawless and her nipples pressed their shape deep into my brain.

"Yesss," Mykonos continued, as if speaking to himself, "Everybody wants her."

Then the waitress came to our table. She was stunning. She was standing so close I could see the fine blonde hairs on her tummy. Her eyes were clear and blue, and her smile was truly happy, as if she was having the time of her life waiting tables. The slit of her sarong revealed lotion-glistening thighs all the way up to the yellow bikini bottom she wore under her silky wrap.

"Hello, my dear," Mykonos said to the waitress, "We'll have three pitchers of beer and some more fish tacos for

Dimitri," nodding toward our friend who looked up from his plate and smiled.

"Is that all?" asked the waitress.

"That's it for now," Mykonos answered.

As she walked away, I watched her until she disappeared through the door next to the stage.

"Poor Paco," Mykonos said, gazing out toward the beach where the volleyball game was in progress. "He thinks he can play. Look at him. He thinks he's really good."

Paco was a lot better at volleyball than I was, and as far as I knew, he was a lot better than Mykonos, too.

"All puffed up, thinking he looks so good. One day, Paco is going to find his heart. And then…" Mykonos trailed off, smiling as if he knew the punchline to a joke that was yet to come.

When a busboy brought our beer, Mykonos filled his glass and raised it. "To the Great One."

"To the Great One," we all joined in, raising our beer, and then drinking.

I kept looking for the waitress.

We drank beer, snacked a bit, and relaxed, as the afternoon grew long. Paco finally finished playing and returned to our table. Mykonos greeted him.

"You're a fine player, Paco."

"Yeah, I'm not bad. Used to be better. I used to play in college and…"

"Would you like a beer, my friend," Mykonos interrupted.

"Sure," Paco answered, as Lemuel filled his glass.

"To the Great One," Paco toasted, raising his glass.

We all raised our glasses, and drank.

"We are all enjoying this fine day together, filled with love, and our friend here has his mind on a whoor," Mykonos said toward me with a raise of his eyebrow. He said the word "whoor" like it rhymed with "tour" whenever he was praising a woman for her radiance, her light, her open-heartedness. For Mykonos, "whoor" meant something very different than the common word "whore." A "whoor" was a vision of light, a goddess.

"Where is she now?" Mykonos asked me, looking directly into my eyes. His eyes were very dark, the deep black of an endless well.

"I don't know. Probably back in the kitchen, I guess."

"You can't feel her now? Hmmm? Are you *bereft* of woman?" He emphasized the word "bereft" to tease me; it was the kind of word I would use, not he.

"No. I'm not *bereft* of women."

"I said *woman*, not women."

I looked into his eyes. He held my gaze without moving. Suddenly, everything stopped. It was as if we were in a movie, and everything froze motionless—the people, the birds, the ocean, all completely still—while Mykonos continued.

"*Breathe her.*"

I couldn't tell if Mykonos said this out loud, or if I was remembering something he had said earlier. I noticed that I had stopped breathing. I began to breathe again. Still, nothing else moved. As I inhaled, a fragrance filled my body with tendrils of love, curling like paisleys deep in my heart. Mykonos held my gaze with his deep black eyes. The bliss of paisley was now almost too much to bear.

And everybody was laughing and talking suddenly, the birds flew and the ocean lapped up on the beach, as Mykonos broke his gaze and reached for his beer.

"Do you think she likes you?" he asked me.

"I don't know."

"She doesn't even know you exist," Mykonos said. "Lemuel, how long has your friend here been obsessed with women?"

"I never thought he was obsessed with women," Lemuel answered.

"Oh, yes. He is obsessed with women, although he doesn't like them."

"He seems to like women to me."

"Not exactly," Mykonos said while pulling back his lips, exposing his crooked teeth. "Do you know what I'm talking about, Dimitri? No, you do not. Look at Dimitri eating. Look at how happy he is."

Mykonos laughed and drank more beer. As usual, I tried to keep up with Mykonos, drinking whenever he did, gulp for gulp. I felt a little woozy. The air was still hot, though it was getting late.

The band climbed up on the stage and began playing. It was typical bar brand music, generic and uninteresting.

"Yes! Right on!" Mykonos began shouting to the band.

I was still thinking about what Mykonos had said to Lemuel. What did he mean that I didn't like women?

"C'mon men," Mykonos said to us. "Let's give the band some energy. They are here to serve us and bring us happiness. Show them you are into it."

"But Mykonos, I'm not into it," Paco said as he read the back of the menu.

"Paco, you're not *into* anything. Have another beer, my friend." Mykonos re-filled his glass.

Paco continued. "I mean it. I don't want to fake it. This music sucks."

Mykonos smiled wide and shook his head in mock disbelief.

He pushed his craggy face forward so his bent nose was inches from Paco's. "This is God," Mykonos said. He paused for a moment, smiling into Paco's face, and then sat back, bursting out with laughter.

"Who the hell am I hanging out with? A mutant, a reject from Shaker Heights, a dolphin, and the Lord of Darkness himself! You guys are unbelievable! This is it! Right now! This is the Divine Vision! It doesn't get more divine than this!"

Mykonos raised his glass high. This time, he didn't say a toast. He touched the air with his beer glass, toasting silently with an unseen guest.

"I don't know. Maybe it's time to go home." Mykonos wondered out loud.

Dimitri chimed in. "We can give the band energy. Alright!" he shouted to the band. "Alright! We love you!"

I cringed. I couldn't believe how naïve and gullible Dimitri seemed.

"Yes!" Mykonos yelled right along with Dimitri. "We're with you!"

The band looked up directly at our table. They smiled and nodded. Mykonos lifted his beer to them, and smiled. "Good job Dimitri."

Paco continued to sulk. He hunched his shoulders and pressed his lips together.

"What's wrong, Paco? You can play volleyball with great energy, but you can't give love to the band?" Mykonos asked.

"But I don't love them. I don't even know them!"

"Ahh. Paco." Mykonos pulled back his lips again and hissed. "Yesss. You don't know them. You can only love. That's all you can *ever* do, Paco. The band is always playing, whether you like them or not. Do you know what I mean? The lady is always showing herself to you, whether you like her or not"—I knew Mykonos was talking to me now—"and all you can do is love. Even if the band doesn't know who you are. Even if the lady doesn't care."

"She's a beautiful whoor, is she not?" Mykonos asked, looking directly into my eyes. I began to feel like I was sinking, being pressed down at my heart into a hole with no bottom, spinning a little, and suddenly the waitress was at our table, refilling our water glasses. She must have come up from behind me.

"Are you having a good day?" Mykonos asked the waitress.

"Yes. It's a little busy. But I like it that way."

"My friend here finds you beautiful," Mykonos said, nodding toward me. I couldn't believe Mykonos had said that.

"Thank you," the waitress said, without a hint of shyness. I thought she must receive compliments all the time.

"It's a beautiful day, isn't it?" Mykonos asked her.

"Really beautiful. I love clear, sunny days."

"You can feel the sunshine in your heart, can't you?"

She stopped filling our glasses and looked at Mykonos for the first time.

"Yes. I guess I can."

"Your heart is very bright, my dear." Mykonos continued, his deep black eyes looking into hers.

She smiled and held gaze with Mykonos. Nobody said a word. Finally, she looked down, swallowed, looked up again at Mykonos, breathed deeply, nodded, and walked off.

"A truly fine whoor, that one."

Everyone lifted their glasses and drank with Mykonos, except Paco.

"Do you have a problem, Paco?" Mykonos asked.

"No."

"Does he have a problem?" Mykonos asked, turning to me.

"Paco doesn't like to be happy."

"That's not true," Paco quickly responded, leaning forward and crinkling his forehead. "I just don't like to lie."

"You think we are lying, is that it, Paco?" Mykonos asked.

"Well, sort of. I mean, you don't even know that waitress, but you treat her like a princess. The band sucks, but you pretend that it's good. Last night, you treated Adrienne like an old friend, but you had never even met her before! I just don't feel like faking it."

"Paco, Paco, Paco," Mykonos said through his teeth. "Why the hell are you alive?"

"I don't know. Maybe I shouldn't be."

"Paco, I think Mykonos is asking why *anyone* is alive," Lemuel suggested.

"Yesss. What does 'alive' mean?"

"I don't know." Paco said, with a shrug.

"Well, what does being alive *feel* like?" Mykonos asked.

"Right now, pretty bad. I feel like you guys are attacking me."

"Paco, look at these strange friends of yours here. They love you. You know it."

"Yeah. I guess so. I just don't want to pretend I'm happy if I'm not. I don't want to pretend that I like the band if I don't."

"Why not?" Mykonos asked as he drank his beer.

"Because I want to be authentic."

Mykonos laughed so suddenly that he spewed beer over Lemuel. Lemuel took off his spotted glasses and wiped them clean with a napkin, smiling.

"Paco," Mykonos continued, "look around you."

Paco straightened his spine and looked around. "Yeah?"

"What do you see?"

"The ocean, the sky, the sand, a bunch of people."

"And what are they doing?"

"I don't know. Whatever they are doing."

"Exactly." Mykonos sat back and swallowed another gulp of cold beer. His gaze was now directed over the ocean, as if he were looking at something far, far away, perhaps just over the horizon. "Volleyball. Women. Fish tacos. You've got to feel her right now, all around you like the colors of a flame, touching you always. Do you know what I mean? You've got to love her, breathe her, feel the truth of her, until she dies. What else are you going to do?"

"That might work for you, but not for me," Paco announced sitting back in his chair.

Mykonos paused and breathed deeply. He put his hand on Paco's thigh and spoke lovingly, "You are not alive for yourself, my friend. You are not here to play volleyball and withhold your love—from us or from Erin—because you don't feel it. You are *alive* as love. This whole place is lit up as love. If you can't feel it, don't punish others for your inability to feel. Loosen up, my friend. Feel the mystery of you and this whole place, breathe the mystery—and then you tell me if this place is other than love. Hmmm? Maybe *you* are living a lie, Paco, not me. Love is the truth—of you and all these other monkeys."

"But I don't *feel* love," Paco said, almost pleading.

"Ahh, yesss." Mykonos sat still for a few minutes, looking far off toward the horizon. Suddenly he smiled hugely, and started to speak with moist eyes. "Have you ever looked closely at a flame, Paco? The reds and yellows are easy to see, but deep in the center of the flame is blue. You can easily avoid the blue, miss it altogether if you just look at the surface colors. But always blue is here, deeper than where your vision stops. Even now, blue." Quietly, Mykonos made a sound I could barely hear, and then sat in silence, still gazing far away.

After a few moments, Mykonos pointed. "Look into the sky. Look deeply. Blue. Look into the ocean. The deeper the water, the bluer it gets. Blue is the color of deep. And beyond everything you can see, deeper than all the things you like or don't like, there is a place where everything is blue, so blue, like water that does not end…" Mykonos stopped himself and smiled.

"I still don't see why I should try to give people love if I don't feel love," said Paco.

"Because, my dear friend, you *are* love. But you are trapped in the colors that possess your eyes and curl around your heart. Feel deeper than your sulk, feel deeper than what you can see, feel into the blue. The waitress, fish tacos, volleyball—everything you can see and know is more shallow than the blue truth."

"And just what is the blue truth, Mykonos?" asked Paco.

"For you, Paco? What is the true blue truth? Whatever sets your heart free. Whatever allows you to feel deeper than things seem. If you want to curl up and pout, Paco, nobody can stop you. But it hurts you and everyone to do so, because it's a lie, and deep down, you know it."

Mykonos turned again to the band. "Yes!" he shouted as the lead singer hit a high note, "Yes! Right on!"

The lead singer looked at Mykonos and smiled. The band began to play with more life. The whole place seemed to come alive, to get brighter.

"Can you feel her now?" Mykonos suddenly turned and asked while gazing deep into my eyes. "Can you feel her alive as everything, or do you still only feel her when she fills your damn glass—or sucks your dick?" he asked me.

"I feel her, Mykonos."

"Yesss. When you are ready, when you embrace her for the sake of the truth of her, you'll know who she really is. Now you only see the tip of her flame, pulling you in and burning you up in all this surface loving, in all these bodies and eating and sexing. She's fantastic! My friends, if you could see her surrendered over, *totally* taken by the Great One where no appearance burns at all, where it is cooler even than blue…

Mykonos smiled and showed his teeth. He reached for his beer, looked at each of us, and laughed. "Perhaps, for now, the blue truth is enough. Hmmm?"

5
Beyond Bondage

∾

"Gia is going to kill you some day," Mykonos said. We were sitting on the sand, looking at the ocean water rolling in. Mykonos and I had been getting together almost every day for a number of years now, and he had decided I needed to learn to surf. He was teaching me to boogie board, which is done lying down on a small body board rather than standing up on a regular surfboard.

"What?" I asked.

"Gia is going to kill you unless she leaves you alone. She loves you so much, you are going to burn up."

Lately, my nose had been bleeding, especially while teaching the workshops on sexuality and spirituality that Mykonos had encouraged me to teach. I would sometimes get a high fever that lasted for several days, with no other symptoms. I went to see several doctors and specialists, but they couldn't find anything wrong with me. Mykonos suggested I had a condition that he called, "Shakti fever." He seemed to think the internal heat was part of a spiritual process. He also thought that Gia—who was a "hot" woman, full of fiery passion and urgent love—might be adding to the heat.

"I know you love her, and she loves you. But this isn't about love, its about a pattern you might not be able to see," Mykonos said. "Come on, let's get in the water."

We walked down the beach to the ocean's edge, lay on our boards in the water, and paddled out beyond where the waves were breaking. Rising up and sinking down with each ocean swell, we relaxed on our boards in silence.

"The water is consciousness," Mykonos said. "Feel it. Everywhere. Hmmm?"

Although we were floating on the ocean, the "water" Mykonos was talking about was obvious. It was as if we were floating, or suspended in, and even made of, *infinite* water, a fullness that felt love-thick yet open. We relaxed without speaking for more than an hour. Then I started to get nervous.

"Well, my friend, are you ready to let go of your relationship with Gia and move on? Are you ready to trust the open water?"

As Mykonos asked his question, my belly and chest tightened. I was stunned, and I immediately felt unwilling to let go of Gia. We were tied together tightly. She and I shared everything. We had been through so much together for more than a decade that I couldn't imagine living without her. We spent plenty of time apart, teaching, traveling, studying with our teachers, but we always knew we would soon come back together, our relationship renewed. She understood me better than anyone, and she trusted me, as I did her, implicitly.

"Do you really think we should move on?" I asked, feeling somewhat disingenuous—I could already feel what Mykonos was getting at.

"Nothing is permanent," Mykonos said. "Let her go, and see if she comes back. You two have been together for a long time. Your love is deep and real, deeper than most people will ever experience in their lives. But you are also identified with each other as a couple. The Peepster,"—Mykonos often called Gia the "Peepster" for some reason—"she is identified with being your partner. She wants to be known as yours. It's important to her. And she idealizes your relationship. She doesn't understand that what she wants from you, no man could give her."

We bobbed up and down on the swells as I felt into what Mykonos was saying, knowing that he had hit upon one of my tightest knots of fear.

"And you, you're afraid to let go of your relationship and be lived by the Great One for real. If you want my gut feeling, it's time for you and the Peepster to trust deeper than the form of your relationship. Let go of each other while you continue to open your hearts and love. Break the old patterns of relating. Mix it up a little. You don't have children to worry about. Why not find out what happens? The future can't be predicted. Maybe you'll come back together as a couple, maybe you won't. But it's time to let go and find out what happens when you open and offer your love without holding onto the past form. That's my gut feeling, if you want it."

Mykonos had never given me such direct advice before. Although he frequently suggested practices to me, he had never offered such strong and specific direction about how to live my life. He always left it up to me to feel what was best, perhaps offering subtle hints as to his feeling. I was surprised by the strength of his direct suggestion—and I felt punched in the belly by the thought of possibly losing my relationship with Gia.

"How often do you and the Peepster teach together," Mykonos asked me.

"Pretty often. Whenever our schedule allows it. Why?"

"Well, I'm not sure it's a good idea to teach together. You are both identified with being a couple, and the public expects that. At least for a while, maybe you should take a break from teaching together."

For years—even before meeting Mykonos—Gia and I had taught together, and we made a great team. My mind was trying to grasp the rightness or not of Mykonos's suggestion, but mostly I felt nauseous and afraid.

Gia and I had recently been feeling a shift deep beneath the surface of our relationship. She and I talked about it at length, but we couldn't put our finger on it. Until Mykonos offered his gut feeling, I hadn't allowed myself to feel how reticent I was to plunge this particular depth. I was letting something slide deep down while riding the luxuriance of a fruitful and fulfilling relationship. Mykonos's suggestion intervened sharply in my laxity.

"Feel the water, my friend," Mykonos said, looking distantly over the horizon. "Endless water. In that endlessness, we all make our cults. Our little cults of relationship give us a sense of purpose, comfort, and safety. We are all going to die, but before that, we do everything we can to have it all make sense, to feel loved, to find our place. But there is no place. Hmmm? There is no place! Just the *room* you find yourself in for the present, and even that can be felt beyond, hmmm?"

The thought of risking my relationship with Gia was tightening my gut, closing in my feelers, so I didn't even notice the ocean and sky—let alone the *room* and the deep space of consciousness that Mykonos was indicating. I was thinking of Gia, about how much I loved her, about our incredible time together. I had expected to be with her for the rest of my life. Even so, Mykonos's force of truth was cutting through my worries, opening me to a deep trust that felt utterly free, even as my body and mind panicked.

"Let her go, my friend. Let everything go, and see what remains, hmmm?"

Mykonos paddled to catch the next wave. I watched the curl of water carry him toward the beach. When his ride finished, he slowly paddled back out toward me, stopping about 20 feet away.

I couldn't tell if his distance signaled that the discussion was over, or if he wanted to be alone. I paddled toward him, slowly. He didn't seem to notice. He looked out over the ocean, facing the horizon where the blue water and the blue sky met. I floated on my board, bobbing up and down with the swells, feeling the openness of the water, my insides still churning in turmoil.

"You should find yourself another woman, and Gia should find herself another man. See what happens."

I was shocked, again, by Mykonos's atypical directness, and I was turned inside out by his suggestion. My abdominal organs felt grabbed and exposed to the ocean's slosh. Mykonos's words seized and revealed the submerged patterns of my bonding with Gia.

I held onto Gia as a precious jewel—perhaps the most precious part of my life. Other people seemed to value our relationship, too. People who attended our workshops often looked to our relationship as an example. I began worrying about the ramifications to others, when Mykonos read my mind.

"Why do you think people come to your workshops?" Mykonos suddenly asked.

"To learn something, to grow, I suppose."

"Yes, but it has nothing to do with what you say. They come because they feel something from you. They feel your openness, your *yogic disposition*," Mykonos said with a smile, crinkling his nose, explaining and chiding me at the same time. "All you and Gia can offer is your integrity as practitioners of love. It's time for you both to live without a safety net, opening to be lived by the Great One, discovering your true form of love as you offer your heart, breath by breath."

I felt into further repercussions of changing the form of our relationship. I felt how my and Gia's families might react. I thought of our friends. Our daily life together. Our intimate discussions. Cuddling. I remembered all the times Gia had stayed with me while I was sick, in the hospital, through every major physical, emotional, and spiritual crisis of my adult life. She had always been with me, through good times and bad, offering me a depth of love, devotion, and wisdom that I had never felt in another woman. Ever. Why would I want to risk that? I would never find another woman like Gia.

"Outside!" Mykonos said, indicating that a large wave was rolling in.

For a while I didn't move. My attention was locked in a cascade of catastrophe and consequence unfolding in my mind. I snapped out of my reverie just in time to duck under the wave, holding my breath until the water passed over me.

"Love is love. Sex is sex. And bondage—even beautiful bondage—is still bondage. Do you understand?" Mykonos asked.

I could feel what Mykonos was talking about, but I didn't want to feel it.

"I remember once, many years ago, when my wife and I were living with my teacher and some of his students," Mykonos recalled, looking out over the horizon. "One night, my teacher knocked on my cabin door. It was late, and I had been sleeping, alone. He was laughing hysterically when I opened the door. I asked him what he wanted, but he just kept laughing, signaling me with his finger to follow him. We walked along the forest trail, past a few cabins, finally stopping outside the window to a cabin of one of my friends. My teacher pressed his ear against the window—the curtain was closed so you couldn't see inside—and then he fell to the ground laughing."

Mykonos paused for a few moments as a set of waves rolled beneath us.

"Finally, I pressed my ear against the window of the cabin," Mykonos continued with his story. "I could hear two people having sex, loudly. The woman, especially, was moaning and screaming in pleasure. And then I realized, it was my wife! My wife was in that cabin having sex with another man. And loving it! She was screaming with pleasure! I remember how offended I was, that my wife could have as much pleasure with another man as with me. And I remember my teacher laughing."

Mykonos smiled for a moment, and then stopped. He turned to look at me with great love and understanding in his eyes.

"Gia and you share a deep love, but maybe it's time to break the cult."

Mykonos rode a wave in toward shore, then paddled back out, and took another wave in. I was too stunned to really get into surfing. I did my best to relax my body in the cool ocean water, draping my arms over the board.

Eventually, Mykonos paddled back out, resting when he was close enough for me to hear him. "Relationship is bondage, unless your love is larger than the cult," Mykonos said, his voice quiet and sweet. "Are you ready to feel open, as endless and object-free as the water? Perhaps not," Mykonos smiled, looking tenderly into my eyes.

He took the next wave in to the shore and I followed him. We set our boards down on the beach and sat on the sand, looking out over the ocean.

A man and woman walked by, hand in hand. A bit down the beach, the couple stopped to embrace and kiss, the waves rolling up the beach, swirling around their ankles.

Mykonos nodded toward them. "Most people never get beyond trying to own each other's love in a kind of contractual bondage. I'm not saying you should have sex with all kinds of people. That would be bondage too—bondage to the vagaries of your desire. When you can stand free and love without ownership, so your entire being is open like water, maybe you choose to be alone or celibate. Maybe you choose to share love in a couple, perhaps raising a family. Maybe you choose to have ten sexual partners. Maybe you are heterosexual or homosexual. Your true form of intimacy must be discovered with real integrity in love."

Mykonos continued looking at the couple, holding each other in the shallows as the waves rolled in and back out into the ocean. "Every person needs to find the true form of their intimacy, their way of opening as love to God through sex—and you can choose to have a deep and loving intimate relationship without any sex at all. Whatever form of love you choose, commit to loving without limit, giving yourself entirely. But when a love relationship becomes a stand-in for utter openness—when you are afraid of losing love—then you bind yourself in clinging, enclosing love in a cult of two, engaging your lover in contracts of fear. When a relationship binds your heart in fear of betrayal, then it isn't an offering of love, it's a trap."

I wondered whether I was ready to live by this truth, which seemed so obvious. Part of me certainly felt that Gia was mine. I felt assured in her devotion. I assumed that she would never be with another man. I took great comfort in knowing that Gia was waiting for me when I was traveling, teaching on the road. I carried the knowledge of our relationship like a life preserver, knowing Gia's love would support me if I began to drown, as it had many times.

Mykonos was asking me to risk the safety of the most loving, intimate, and secure relationship I had ever known. He was suggesting that I let go of the woman who was utterly devoted to me, a woman whom I knew was not only irreplaceable, but unique in the depth of her heart's expression. The woman I loved without doubt.

"You don't have to leave her," Mykonos said. "You should do whatever feels right in your deepest heart. Feel deep as consciousness, open as water, now, and feel how to live with a wide-open heart. Feel how to live as love without bondage. Listen to your heart through your fear, and be willing to take the next step without the slightest idea of what will happen when you do. Live true to your deepest integrity of love, offering your entire life as love, opening moment by moment, without protecting your heart in traps of safety. This freedom is the ultimate discipline, my friend."

As he stood up, Mykonos looked at me with a big smile. "And if some people can't deal with it, fuck 'em."

I went home and talked with Gia about the conversation I had with Mykonos. She agreed entirely with what Mykonos had said, which surprised me at first, but then seemed obvious and inevitable. For a week, we talked about letting go of our relationship and perhaps finding other partners. We often cried, day and night. We loved each other deep and thick, and yet we both felt a basic pattern in our relationship was genuinely shifting. In some ways, in the center of our hearts, nothing would change because our love couldn't change. We felt our love to be unassailable, and also felt it was time to trust love and move on in open-hearted discovery. Neither of us knew what that would entail.

# 6
She Comes in Two

A few nights later, we gathered with Mykonos again in my living room. We were naked. Zelda was dancing to the music of Carlos Santana. Mykonos squinted his eyes slightly.

"You might be able to make it, you hairy fucker," he said, sizing me up, looking up and down my body as I sat on the couch across from him. "It all depends on whether you can sing 'Happy Birthday.'"

"Happy Birthday?" I wondered, still sad in my heart, trying to let go of Gia.

"Yes," Mykonos continued. "Can you see everyone, meet everyone, feel everyone, as if you were singing 'Happy Birthday' to them?"

I smiled, thinking of singing 'Happy Birthday' to everyone I met. Just then, Zelda danced her way toward me, shaking her body, sweat glistening. She came right up to me and thrust her hips in my face. Mykonos laughed.

I looked up into Zelda's eyes and sang loudly, "Happy birthday to you, happy birthday to you, happy birthday dear Zelda, happy birthday to you!"

"Yesss," Mykonos hissed. "To love everyone is the only way to live. Give everyone your love as if you were singing 'Happy Birthday' to them, you know what I mean? Why would you want to live any other way? Hmmm?"

Zelda came closer until her crotch was inches from my nose. I looked up into her shining eyes. My Happy Birthday song seemed to give her even more energy. She licked her lips, smiled, and lowered herself so she could hump my thigh, laughing.

"You might be able to make it," Mykonos said to me, "if you could only love without fear, my friend."

Mykonos was right. I was afraid. Gia was in the other room. I was wondering what would happen if she saw me with Zelda.

"Do you trust love, or not?" Mykonos asked. "Are you willing to love completely and follow love wherever it takes you? Or does your pecker get in the way? You know what I mean?"

Zelda began kissing my neck as she rubbed her crotch against my leg. I could feel the smooth warmth of her inner thighs and the moist trail of her desire. I smelled her, felt her, saw her, and I was afraid.

"Happy birthday to you, happy birthday to you!" Mykonos laughed as he sang to me, relaxing my heart more open. "She's dancing for you. Do you like it?"

"Yes."

"Of course you do. She's a fine lady. She's alive and *she's dancing for you*. She's all around you. Hmmm?"

I looked over at Mykonos and our eyes met. Suddenly, the scene faded, as if the colors and sound of a movie spread to white, Mykonos's dark eyes holding deep in the center. His still gaze reached into my heart and took my core to feel. Zelda was grinding on my thigh and the music played, but shapes were barely noticed. A silent, motionless certainty of love welled up from my heart and saturated all full joy. Warmth spread into my belly, groin, and legs. My genitals felt full. Mykonos nodded very slightly, the white faded to color, and noticing began again.

Zelda laughed. Mykonos turned to Layla, sitting on the couch next to him. "I feel it in my genitals, don't you Layla?"

Layla smiled and looked down toward her feet. Mykonos put his hand on her thigh. Layla put her hand on top of his, and she looked at Mykonos fetchingly.

"Mm-hmm! Just as I thought. My little porkie pie here is feeling a bit *aroused*. Layla, why don't you get up and dance for us?"

Layla was slow to move.

"Show me, ma!" Mykonos shouted and smiled. "Show me where you are *really* at!"

Layla jumped up and began dancing alone. Then she took Zelda's hand, pulling her up off my leg to dance together.

I could hear people in other parts of the house talking and laughing. Mykonos and I sat on our couches, watching Layla and Zelda dance. Their breasts and bellies pressed together as they kissed and whispered. Laughing wildly, they released each other's grasp and spun around like whirling dervishes, their brown hair flying. I couldn't tell if they were dancing for us or if they didn't even notice our existence.

"There are always two," said Mykonos matter-of-factly. "Wherever women come together, there are always two. Women come in pairs. Do you know what I mean?"

I didn't really know what Mykonos meant, so I didn't answer.

"When you die, my friend, look straight ahead. Do not look to the left," Mykonos said, looking at Layla, "or to the right," he continued, nodding his head toward Zelda. "Do not be distracted, or you will be sucked right back to a place like this," he said, looking around the room.

"Your body grows older. One day, when you get to be around my age," Mykonos said with a half-smile, "you'll look in the mirror and see an old man. The body ages, but you still feel young inside. Your mind, it stays around 18 years old or so. You're still looking at women like a teenager, but your body isn't the same body. You know what I mean?"

"Yes."

"You're looking at all the fine ladies like we have here," nodding toward Zelda and Layla, dancing nakedly, "but your body is getting ready to die. And when you die, the body drops off, and something like your mind continues. So even after you die, you have a kind of fascination with sex, just like you do now, just like old men do. Even though their body is old, they still think like they are young men, they still think about women. And so, after you die, you get sucked right back to a place like this, a sex place, because that is what is on your mind."

Mykonos remained silent for a few minutes, as we watched the two women dance. Then, Mykonos turned to me, leaned forward, and gazed deeply into my eyes.

"And so, never look to the left or right. When you die, go straight into the light in the center. Don't be distracted by one side or the other."

Just then, Layla sat on the couch next to Mykonos, pressed her breasts against his arm, and whispered something into his hear. Mykonos turned toward her. Layla smiled and said, "You're turning to the left. I got you."

Mykonos smiled. Then he pulled back his lips, inhaling with a hiss through his exposed front teeth as he turned back toward me.

"Yesss. And so I am here, with you people. My teacher has shown me many times what happens when you get lost in the lady, and here I am. What can I say?"

Layla continued to press against Mykonos's arm while Zelda sat down to his other side.

"It's not *that* bad, is it?" Zelda asked, nibbling Mykonos's neck and laughing.

"Always two, my friend," Mykonos said looking at me, more sheepish than I had ever seen him. "She always comes in two." And with that said, he stood up and walked off toward the bathroom, leaving me with the two ladies.

I didn't know what to do. Two naked women, quite beautiful, and very sexy. I looked at one, then the other, and imagined that I was dead. Looking to the left and the right. Distracted by ladies. By two. By their promise. Of what?

They started chatting with one another as I looked at them. I tried to feel what I wanted, *why* I wanted them. I wanted to touch them, to take them, to merge with them. I wanted to lose myself in their beauty, their fragrance, their light. I wanted to open with them and feel them open. To be one with them.

Cold water poured down my back.

"Christ!" I shouted, jumping up. I turned to see Paco standing behind me, holding a glass of ice water.

"Sorry, man. It's dripping. Just thought you might want some water."

I took the water and drank it. I was very thirsty. It was a hot night.

Mykonos walked back into the room. "What do you think Paco? Would you give up women for unchanging, perfect bliss? Would you give up everything to be consciousness only? Are you willing to give it all up, *everything*? Or do you prefer ladies to nothing at all?"

"I definitely prefer ladies, Mykonos," Paco said quite seriously.

"Yesss. And so it goes. Here we are, in this *room*, in this *place*, again and again, with our strong preference for *something*. For the left or the right. Sometimes the left *and* the right." Mykonos looked over at Zelda and Layla who were now on the couch. "This is about as low as you can get, and still awaken as consciousness. There are more sublime places, but this is about as dark and dense as the Great One can incarnate and still possibly awaken as Itself. We need more beer. Is there any more beer here?"

"I'll go check," I said, and walked to the kitchen.

Gia was in the kitchen, kneeling on the floor in front of naked Lemuel, my best friend.

My gut immediately tightened and sickened. Gia and I knew we would be testing our limits with Mykonos, but the sight of her with another man shocked me. I breathed deeply in and out of my belly, as Mykonos had taught me. I felt Gia and Lemuel. I felt the whole kitchen. I practiced to feel the whole scene without pulling away, without creasing my gut in loathing.

As I practiced breathing and opening, I remembered the first time I met Mykonos's teacher. I was with a group of people, and we were all sitting in front of him. He would look into each of our eyes, one person at a time. When he looked into my eyes, I immediately wanted to kill him. Visions of stabbing him, cutting him open, dismembering him, and eviscerating him continued to arise as I gazed into his eyes.

His face did not move. He sat, wide open, staring into my eyes. After many minutes these horrific visions passed. He looked into my eyes as if he was I. There was no sense of another person looking into my eyes, only love loving love. I relaxed completely. My entire being opened, like a vast sheet that had seemed forever crinkled, finally relaxing wide, as it always had been in truth, love without a crease.

He was this love. I was this love. All things, everyone, appeared as transparent forms in this one ocean of love. I felt I was enlightened.

And instantly his face grimaced in pain. His body remained perfectly motionless, but his face contorted in an agonized scowl, which I felt in my heart. I had creased the sheet of love, and he felt it acutely. I *was* the creasing in the sheet, proud of my realization, curling back on myself, smugly, to know my own achievement.

Were it not for the pained scowl on his face, I wouldn't have noticed that I was folding love in needful tension, pinching infinity's heart, creasing openness to make an event of noticing myself. I wouldn't have felt the suffering I created by needing to feel myself feeling myself, reflectively knowing my own achievement. But his face so visibly reflected my curled selfing that I could easily notice it, feel what I was doing, and relax open.

I was in awe of this magnificently vulnerable man. He seemed perfectly open and at ease, and yet more sensitive to my heart's response than I was.

As I opened again without needing to feel the event of accomplishment, his face relaxed. His gaze was love without the slightest separation. I felt alive as love, as his love, as openness without end. Everything was the living openness of love. I felt that finally I had achieved spiritual realization. I couldn't wait to tell Gia. And again his face contorted in pain.

This went on for about 15 minutes of excruciating precision. I would relax open as love without difference, alive as the unbroken body of reality, and he was that love. Then, I would try to claim achievement, curling back onto myself to notice that I had opened, and he would scowl, his heart seemingly crushed by my self-curl. He was more susceptible to my most intimate doings than I was!

I remembered his vulnerability as I stood in the kitchen, watching Lemuel and Gia together, creasing my heart, closing the openness of love. Even as I practiced to relax my belly and breathe deeply, my heart continued to contract in reaction to Gia and another man. My mind rushed. Hadn't I been special to her, somehow? Didn't she love me in a way she didn't love other men? How could she enjoy herself with Lemuel? He hasn't gone through the ups and downs, the special moments as well as the hellish times, that Gia and I had been through over the years.

"What do we have here?" Mykonos bellowed as he walked into the kitchen. "I see you are distracted by the left and the right, hmmm? Let me tell you a little secret, my friend. This is merely a vision, you know? Your best friend and Gia—enjoying herself *immensely*, I might add. And why not? Would you want to limit her pleasure, her love? Do you think she should only love your hairy ass? Do you feel," Mykonos paused, looking to the side, smiling, looking back at me, and grinning widely, "do you feel *betrayed*?"

I did feel betrayed. By Gia. By Lemuel. By Mykonos. By everything. I was ready to leave. I wanted my life back the way it used to be.

Mykonos kept looking into my eyes, and I felt his teacher's infinite heart filling me. Like a balloon, I felt a force of fullness opening through me, relaxing my clench, uncreasing my need to know I was special, or even separate. Without breaking eye contact, Mykonos made a very tiny gesture of his head toward Gia and Lemuel. I looked and saw Gia crying. Lemuel was looking straight into my eyes with real love.

All tension fell away. Our bodies felt swelled by love. Everything—the walls, the floor, even the air—felt like a shimmering open of thick water, swelling open as love alive.

"Yesss," Mykonos said quietly. "This vision, this *room*, comes and goes. You either open as love, or you close and suffer. Every thing will betray you. Your woman and friends will betray you. Your own body will betray you. Your entire life as you know it will one day disappear. Are you opening or closing? That is the only question no matter what appears. This is nothing," Mykonos said while moving his head in the direction of Gia and Lemuel. "It gets a lot worse than this. A *lot* worse. Could you open now if a battalion were skewering your body with bayonets? If babies' heads were being crushed under the enemy's feet?"

Mykonos stopped talking and the room was quiet. Suddenly, it was as if we were under water. A pressure came upon us, pressing down through our heads, down through our hearts. A bliss pressed into us, and we all felt it. Gia made a soft moan. I couldn't help but open deeper.

"Yesss. You can feel it pressing down on your beater. Keep opening and take it deep. Take it into you like a woman takes her lover. You can be afraid, or you can open and find out what happens when you take it so deep you are loved to death."

I no longer felt the sharp sense of betrayal that had previously clenched my gut. The thick water pressed gently down into our hearts, into our whole bodies, opening us, living us, living the entire *room* open.

"You love Lemuel, as a friend, don't you?" Mykonos asked Gia.

"Yes."

"You know he thinks his pecker is small."

"Well…" Gia began.

"Yesss," Mykonos cut in. "There is only bliss, but Lemuel is afraid his pecker is too small. Look at that little thing."

We all looked at Lemuel's penis. The sense of being underwater was overwhelmingly pleasurable, and Lemuel looked down at himself, smiling.

"You don't need a dick to open a woman to God, Lemuel," Mykonos said. "You just have to open yourself to God. You've got to open deep yourself, Lemuel, and then you can open your woman deep. You know what I mean?"

Lemuel looked up at Mykonos.

"No. You don't," Mykonos laughed. "You're a beautiful man, Lemuel. You've got face."

We all looked at Lemuel's face. He was beautiful.

"Gia, isn't Lemuel a good looking man?"

"Yes, he is. He's very handsome."

"You can feel him afraid, and you want to suck his dick, right? You feel compassion for him."

"I know I can help him open."

"Exactly," Mykonos said, turning to me. "Gia wants to open a man's heart."

Saturated through by the thick water, heavy with bliss, ballooned out smooth and open, my need to feel special felt thin. Sex was love between bodies. I smiled.

"Just what I thought," said Mykonos. "You might just make it. But you've got to let go of this sex thing, you know? It's just sex. It can be sublime when done as love…"

"Every moment is sex, sublimed as love," I said without thinking.

"Wow!" Mykonos feigned shock. "Yes, indeed. Every moment *is* sex. If you want to make a big deal about whose genitals you try to own, that's your business. But you can feel love, openness, now, can't you? Pressing into you? Opening as you?"

"Yes," I answered.

"Let it open you all the way. Just relax open as the weight of water presses down on your beater. Open your head like a cup, receive it down through you, breathe it open, and be lived by the Great One. Be lived by the love pressing down into you. Be lived as love's force. Help everyone to open and be lived as love. Help Gia and Lemuel live as love. That's what we are here for. Open as love, and this place dissolves as love. Otherwise, this place is a kind of hell, and you feel betrayed, by your woman, by your little pecker," Mykonos looked at Lemuel's crotch, "by everything."

Zelda and Layla walked into the room.

"What's going on?" Layla asked.

"We are contemplating Lemuel's pecker," Mykonos answered.

Zelda walked over to Lemuel and took him in her hand. She examined his penis, looked up, and said, "He seems fine to me!"

Gia and Zelda got on their knees before Lemuel, and Mykonos motioned me to follow him into the other room.

Paco was standing in front of the stereo, reading various CD covers.

"You see," Mykonos said, looking at Paco, "we are all paying attention to something. But what is *before* attention?"

Mykonos picked up a pillow and tossed it so it bonked Paco on the head.

"What the fuck?" Paco turned toward us.

"Have you become an old man, Paco?" Mykonos asked.

"What do you mean?"

"I mean, have you *settled in*?"

"I don't know what you are talking about."

"Paco, my friend, what are you doing with your life?"

"I don't know."

"I wish you didn't. But you *do* know, Paco. What is the purpose of your life, such as it is?"

"To grow, I guess."

"You guess? That, my friend, is your problem. You are like an old man, looking forward to your next shit."

"I don't know what you're talking about."

"Open your heart now!" Mykonos yelled. "What are you waiting for? Hmmm? What are you doing with your attention that is so psychotically riveting?"

"I'm looking at CD's, man. Is that OK?"

"Paco, everything is OK. But is OK good enough for you? Have you become an old man?"

"Hey, I'm just looking at some CD's. I want to see what music we have here."

"You see," Mykonos said, looking at Paco but talking to me, "it's all about attention. You can be full of bliss, open as water without end, or you can worry about your *relationship*, you know? You can be looking at CD's, and forget the vast mystery of the Great One. You've got to keep your cup open, you know? Let go of the need to think-think-think, relax open your head, receive the water down into your heart, open all the way down your body until your body is this whole place. Let this *room* be what it is. It's God, you know, all of this, but if you don't open, it's just narrowed attention, seemingly locked in a *room* of things. One thing after another. Right Paco?"

"Yeah, I suppose so."

"Nothing ever really makes a difference," Mykonos said, turning to me. "You know that, don't you?"

"Yes."

"Well then, what are we going to do with your friend Paco?" Mykonos said while nodding his head toward Paco, who at this point looked like he was about to throw a fit.

"I think he should dance with Layla."

"Excellent! Dancing. We should all be dancing."

Paco put on some new music. Everyone came in from the kitchen and we all danced together.

"One day you will be puking your guts out, dying," Mykonos said to me loudly over the music as we danced. "That moment won't be any different from this one."

Mykonos danced with his arms up in the air. He showed his teeth and moved his hips like a drunken street thug. He sung off key to the music.

"Shake it, ma!" Mykonos yelled toward Zelda, who seemed to be getting tired. "Dance for love! Dance for God! Dance for fuck!"

I looked over at Gia, who was dancing with Lemuel. I could feel the part of me that wanted her to acknowledge a specialness between us.

"Let her go!" Mykonos shouted. "Let her go and see if she comes back. And remember, she always comes in two!"

And at that Mykonos started dancing wildly, closing his eyes and gyrating his hips like a maniac.

7
Love's Wound

∽

Gia and I had just pulled into the driveway and were sitting in the car.

"I think you should be in relationship with Rebecca," she told me.

Rebecca was an attractive woman we had recently met. Gia's abrupt suggestion took me aback. Tension gripped my body—although for the previous few days I had also thought about Rebecca as a possible partner.

"Why Rebecca?" I asked, feeling very surreal.

"I think she can offer you the kind of energy you need," Gia said, her face pained but sincere.

Together, Gia and I felt into this possibility for a few days, and we talked about it extensively. Finally, I called Rebecca on the phone and asked if she would stop by for a visit. Rebecca and I were only acquaintances—I assumed she would find my invitation out-of-the-blue.

"I'll stop by after work," she said.

When she came to the house, I sat at the kitchen table with her and told her why I had invited her over.

"So, Gia and I are going to experiment with having new intimate partners. We are about to move to another city and teach for a few months. Would you like to come with us and try being my intimate partner?"

This felt very, very strange to me. I was asking a woman to be my intimate partner while living in the same house as Gia and the other people who help teach with us. To my surprise, Rebecca told me she had dreamt about this a few nights earlier.

"Will I have to have sex with you?" she asked.

"No. Maybe. I don't know. This whole thing is new to me. I really don't know how it will turn out. If sex feels like the right thing, we'll do it. If not, we won't. It's your choice. It's our choice. This is unknown territory to me."

"Ok. I'd like to try it," Rebecca said. "I'll have to give notice at my job, put my stuff in storage, and rent out my house."

And that was that. We had never had a one-to-one conversation before, and now Rebecca was moving in.

I remembered Mykonos once telling me about the different kinds of relationships.

"We are bound to objects," Mykonos said while we were in a small sushi restaurant eating lunch. While chewing, he motioned with his head toward a table nearby. Two men and two women sat at the table, nibbling at their food and talking. The men both had long hair and earrings, and one of the men had tattoos on his arm. The women were tanned and athletic looking.

"Those boys are *lost*," Mykonos said. "Lost in women."

Mykonos ate another piece of sushi and washed it down with a sip of green tea. A few pieces of rice remained on his lower lip, but he didn't seem to notice.

"Mykonos, you have some rice on your lip."

He wiped his mouth with a napkin and ate some more sushi, leaving more rice on his lips. I didn't bother to tell him.

"Those women have one thing on their mind. Look at them all prettied up. They spend *hours* preparing themselves for men every day. Without a man's adoration, they feel worthless."

Mykonos used his chopsticks to pick up a piece of tempura, which fell back to the plate just before he got it in his mouth. He picked it up with his fingers and ate it.

"And look at those two boys," Mykonos said, although the "boys" were probably in their early 40's. "All shiny and smiley. Chatting like women."

Mykonos suddenly looked at me and said, "You know what I mean, don't you? There's nothing wrong with women…"

Mykonos loved women—truly *appreciated* women—more than any man I had ever met. He didn't need to add his cautious comments, but he seemed to feel it necessary.

"I know what you mean, Mykonos."

"Those men don't know their *death*, that's what I mean. Women *are* life, you know? But when a man gets lost in life without knowing his death, then he is no longer a man. You know what I mean?"

"Yes."

"Look at those two sorry fuckers. Carrying on like fish in a tank, proud of their little pebbles and seaweed, puffing out their gills. They haven't the slightest fucking idea how tiny their world is, how they are dependent on a million things that could go wrong and they would be dead, just like that. All some kid has to do is knock over the tank, you know? Meanwhile, they are staring at some tits, hoping for some pussy, chatting like they cared about the conversation. They can't wait to go home, jerk off, maybe watch a little TV."

I looked over at the table. The four of them were laughing and talking.

"They're singles, and all of them are hoping to get laid. Maybe settle down in a good relationship. Have some kids. Of course, there's nothing wrong with any of that," Mykonos said with a smile, and I remembered that he had a daughter in college. "But it's never enough. Those guys will be looking at their girlie magazines, or maybe have a mistress. Those women will long for their man to love them more. Maybe they'll have an affair, or maybe they'll just eat and buy dresses. Eventually, they'll resign themselves to a tolerable arrangement, or get divorced and start again. It doesn't really matter. If you are bound to objects—even people you truly love—then you suffer, because they can't deliver what you want from them."

"Mykonos, you've been married for twenty years."

"Yesss," Mykonos said, hissing through his teeth, "yes I have. But because of my teacher, I've also gotten to know the laughing mama. You know, the big lady who doesn't give a shit about any of my objections. She shot me up in Vietnam, she laughs as my body ages, she'll be laughing when I die. I'm also married to my wife—but that's a whole 'nuther thing. In truth, my wife and I are each married to the Great One. We don't expect our personal relationship with each other to make us happy—we don't expect *anything* to make us happy. You are either open—which is happiness itself—or you are closing down and suffering. Those people over there," Mykonos nodded toward the nearby table, "don't understand that life is brief and all objects—and relationships—vanish."

Mykonos looked at me as he spoke. "You know, I've had my share of women. It doesn't matter how old or young, how sweet or mean, you are either doing the yoga, or you are not. You are either opening to the Great One through your sexing and talking and spending time together, or you are building in suffering, setting yourself up for disappointment, always about to be betrayed, one way or the other."

Mykonos finished the sushi on his plate and sat back. "Those women, they're going to go home and dream of a good man. Those boys, they're going to fantasize about fucking young women for the rest of their lives. And by the time the ladies are saggy and wrinkled and the men are too old to care, it'll be too late. They won't have the energy to open beyond their shriveled concerns for a better life. A day without too much pain will be good enough. And when they start dying, they'll be horrified. All the relationships in the world won't help them then. It'll all just disappear—every person, every object, every moment of their lives will fade—and be forgotten like a dream."

One of the women at the table began to show the men a new turquoise and silver ring she was wearing.

"If a man can't feel his death, then he drifts into the things of life like he's getting lost in a movie. He forgets where the *room* he sees really is. He loses touch with the openness of consciousness. Day after day passes, money comes and goes, women come and go, and so what? Maybe you change diapers, maybe you change the world. It all disappears. It's good to live fully, you know. But while you are living—while you eat and fuck and do what you can to help others—you've got to understand that the laughing mama doesn't give a shit and death is the ground of your life, just as sleep is the ground of waking. At the end of a day, at the end of a life, no matter what you've done, you drift into another place. And the laughing mama's there, too. And so is death, the place beyond appearance."

The waitress came, and I paid the bill. On the way out of the restaurant, I looked back at the four people talking at the table. I imagined their lives coming and going.

Mykonos spoke as we walked to the car. "It starts with 's' and ends with 'x' and rhymes with 'sex.' Nobody is willing to feel the bliss of the Great One because they are wrapped up in sex, or wishing they were. I say, better to go through it all the way. If you are going to fuck, better to fuck open to God, leaving nothing. Then, when you die, nothing is left undone, unopen. No stone is unturned to God. No regrets. You've done it all, and you know it goes nowhere but where you are right now, in the boundless nowhere of the infinity of fuck, where something is arising, but you don't know what it is, do you Mr. Jones?" Mykonos said with a poor imitation of Bob Dylan's voice. "Everything is utter chaos—alive as love but going nowhere that fulfills—so you bind yourself to objects, to relationships, to feel that your life means something, that you have something to show for it, and that somebody loves you."

I was going to spend a few months teaching while living with both Gia and Rebecca. I didn't want to lose Gia's love. I was still holding on to her, hoping I could maybe have a relationship with Rebecca without losing Gia. I was definitely "bound" to Gia as Mykonos had described. I also could feel my sexual attraction to Rebecca. She was new, a shiny "object" for me to look forward to possessing. I felt caught by both sides of the trap that Mykonos talked about, unwilling to let go of the love that Gia and I had created together, desiring the possibilities and newness with Rebecca, and afraid I might end up with nothing.

Gia and Rebecca were both very beautiful. I felt full and proud that I was living with two women. Even though I was supposed to move on from Gia, we were more like a threesome, and I felt wealthy with women. I could also feel, as

Mykonos suggested, that I was using the affection and flesh that now surrounded me to pad myself from the stark freefall of utter surrender, from the nothingness of deep, open being.

One night, the three of us made love together. I looked into Gia's eyes. She was so deep, so wise. I could feel her commitment to God, as well as her devotion to me. I felt so at ease with her, so at home. I loved her without a trace of doubt. And yet, my body did not respond as a man's does to a *woman*. Ever since I began to experience internal overheating—the fevers, nosebleeds, and heart arrhythmias—I found Gia's physical presence to be sometimes irritating—not emotionally, but physically.

She didn't have to say or do anything specific, simply the heat of her gaze, the passion of her touch, and the urgency of her love was enough to chafe my nervous system, turning me off sexually. Previous to my bout of "Shakti fever," as Mykonos called it, I loved hot, spicy Thai and Mexican food. I enjoyed staying outside in the sun for hours. Now, I couldn't tolerate spicy food at all, and five or ten minutes in the sun was all I could handle. Likewise, Gia's passionate demeanor, which I had previously cherished and found exciting, now felt like too much, even though my love for her had not lessened one iota.

Looking into Gia's eyes, I felt her pain. She knew I loved her deeply—there was no question of that. But she could also feel my body's reticence to combine with her energy. On the other hand, when I turned to Rebecca—whose disposition was very cool, calm, and laid-back to an extreme—my body desired her energy greatly. Gia felt, and suffered, my desire for Rebecca's energy. Particularly when the three of us were being sexual together, Gia felt hurt, Rebecca held back in deference to the deep love she could feel between Gia and me, and I was like a kid in a candy shop where all the candy bit me back when I tried to take a taste.

Whether Mykonos knew what his suggestion would bring about or not, the situation was fine-tuned to promise and frustrate my desire for just about every "object" to which I was bound. The most valuable "thing" in my life—Gia, and the love we shared—was suddenly threatened. The pattern of our comfortable bond had been taken apart, and I doubted it would, or could, ever be put back together again. I could love her, and she could love me, but our sense of "home" was shattered—unless open love itself was our home, a love without expectation or personal ownership.

Rebecca turned out to be exactly what I desired and needed energetically. She was so serene and graceful that I reveled in her energy. She healed me, and turned me on. She inspired me. Of course, she was not experienced in practicing love. I wasn't used to being with a woman who couldn't simply open and connect like Gia could so deeply, although Rebecca's cool demeanor rejuvenated me profoundly.

Gia and I could connect our deep hearts in almost any moment, yet my body could no longer embrace her fully. Rebecca and I could connect our bodies deeply and revel in energetic richness, yet her heart was reluctant to open, and she left me feeling alone.

I now had two women, but found that I was more alone than ever. I also found that I preferred being alone. Dealing with the multiplied emotional melee was, for me, something akin to a nightmare. Gia was explosively jealous that I sexually desired Rebecca. Rebecca was icily envious of the depth of love that I shared with Gia. Given my own tendencies, I would rather not deal with any of it—a weakness Mykonos often pointed out—and here we were tangled in a maelstrom of emotional and sexual turbulence.

Looking into Gia's eyes while we made love, her emotional pain was excruciating. We both cried. We held each other. Our relationship was over as we knew it. And yet, our love for each other was unperturbed. Our hearts were ripped open, ragged, bleeding, and raw with love's tragedy.

We telephoned Mykonos.

"Hello," Mykonos answered.

"Hello, Mykonos. I'm here with Gia, and…"

"How is the Peepster?"

"She's not doing real well. Neither of us are…"

"Mm-hmm. You've got your other girlfriend there as well?"

"She's here, but not in the room with us."

"And what *room* are you in?" Mykonos asked.

I couldn't help but smile. Here we were in some love-drama-tragedy and Mykonos instantly evaporated all heaviness into spacious humor.

"Happy Birthday, Mykonos," I said with a bit of happiness.

"Yesss. Happy Birthday to you, too. Now, what kind of mess have you gotten yourself into?" Mykonos laughed.

"Well, …" I hesitated while trying to summarize the current state of affairs.

"She is all around you, my dear," Mykonos interjected, "and you are either able to open or you are closing down. She—the laughing mama—doesn't care one way or the other. She doesn't care if you live or die. She certainly doesn't give a damn about you and the Peepster. The pain in your heart? Feel it. Love is a wound, my friend, a wound that never heals."

My eyes watered as I felt the hurt in my heart without closing. My breath deepened and I looked at Gia, who was also crying. God I loved her.

"Feel the wound of love," Mykonos said. "Learn to live open, wounded, loving. You can't hold onto Gia forever. Be willing to feel the wound now, and love. If you never see the Peepster again, or if you spend the rest of your life with her, anything less than living heart-open is protecting your heart from real love now, a deep love that never ceases, never closes, never waits, even while you hurt. Love Gia, let her go and love her, keep your heart open, aching, churning in the wound of love that never heals, and discover what happens."

I felt the open rawness of my heart's hurt. I loved Gia. My heart wanted to own her, or else to close to her and turn away. I didn't want to suffer the pain of letting her go and losing her while my heart remained open and hurt. I breathed and practiced to stay open, feeling, loving, even though it hurt. Then my mind kicked in. I began to doubt what I was doing.

I confessed my fears to Mykonos. "I'm afraid I'm making a big mistake, trying to let go of Gia."

"Maybe you are, maybe you aren't. You don't know, and I don't know. You can never know. All you can do is open and act from your deepest love. What does your gut say?"

"My gut says...that it is time to move on." I couldn't believe I said that. I couldn't describe why I felt this way, but it felt deeply true. I didn't want it to be true, but it was the deepest truth I could feel.

"And your heart?"

"My heart loves Gia more than ever."

"Good. That is the best time to move on. My friend, it's time to walk the walk. Now let me talk with the Peepster."

Gia got on the phone. She was weeping and talking, but by the time she hung up, she was smiling through her tears.

We embraced. The front of our bodies softened and pressed into each other. Our hearts were beating hard and our breath became one. Our skin and bones melted and our bodies merged as one open love.

Rebecca walked into the room.

I could feel my body and heart harden slightly. Why was I afraid to love Gia in front of Rebecca? Why was I afraid to love anyone at anytime? I eased back to opening, feeling my body inside the *room* loving these other bodies and also feeling open outside the *room*, opening as the deep space of consciousness. My heart and body relaxed. I breathed deeply with Gia and looked into her eyes. The feeling of tragedy dissipated, leaving only a deep love, wounded to be sure, but also eternal. Gia and I were open as love. Our history together might be ending, but our memory together was lush.

We released each other, and Gia looked at Rebecca. Rebecca looked away for a moment, then looked back into Gia's eyes. They both started crying, and Gia walked to Rebecca, embracing her. They held each other for a few moments, and then Gia left the room.

Rebecca's eyes were wet and her face was flushed. I walked toward her and stood close to her. She seemed a little guarded.

"I don't want to stand between you and Gia. I don't want to be the 'other' woman," she said.

"You aren't the 'other' woman," I answered.

"Then, what am I?"

I didn't know quite how to answer. It was all too new. I wasn't sure exactly what our relationship was. I wasn't even sure what I wanted our relationship to be. I was still afraid to totally let go of Gia, and continuing as a threesome was far too painful for everybody—especially because I was so ambiguous.

I remembered Mykonos once teaching Paco and Erin how to go deeper than ambiguity in relationship. Erin was feeling hurt that Paco didn't know what he truly wanted with her.

"You've been with Erin for how long now?" Mykonos asked Paco.

"Six or seven months, I guess," Paco answered.

"But I never know if he is going to be with me another day," Erin added.

"Is he totally with you now?" Mykonos asked Erin.

"Well, that's not what he feels like. I don't know if he really wants to be with me. He's wishy-washy. He's driving me crazy."

"But I *don't* know if I want to be with you," Paco explained. "Would you rather that I faked it and pretended that I was certain?"

Mykonos grimaced and sat back in his chair.

"Paco, Paco, Paco. Do you have a heart?"

"Yes. Why?"

"Use it," Mykonos said. "You are in your head. Your head is filled with doubt. Your head *is* doubt. Your brain is cramped as you think about the possibilities. Being with Erin is one possibility. Being with another woman is also possible. Maybe you should be alone. You are waffling in doubt, hmmm?"

"Yeah. I like Erin a lot. I love her, really. I just don't know if she is right for me. And, yeah, sometimes I think about being with other women. I mean, she probably thinks about being with other men, too."

"Yes, she probably does," Mykonos replied. "And she will always be filled with conflict. The entire world, including every body and mind, is a realm of opposites. You and

Erin are filled with contradictions. There is nothing singular about you. Today you love Erin, and you feel pretty certain. Tomorrow you may meet someone else and feel pretty certain that you don't love Erin. Maybe what you call love isn't even love, hmmm? The mind is an idiot box, filled with possibilities, each of which leads you in a different direction. You are reduced to weakness if you live in your mind, which always expresses doubt and ambiguity."

"But my doubt is real. I really don't know what I want."

"My friend, you don't know anything! You don't know if you are going to be alive in ten minutes. You don't know what you are going to say next. You don't know if I'm going to punch you or kiss you, and you sure as hell don't know if Erin is the 'right one.'"

"So what am I supposed to do?"

"Relax your mind, first. Feel open, like you would feel warm wind blowing on your skin. Feel Erin, feel the world. Feel everything, and open. Open as everything, as the entire *room*. Allow everything to arise as it does, and feel into depth. Feel deeper than your thoughts. Your thoughts, and the rest of the world, arise in opposing pairs. She, the world, always comes in two. 'She loves me, she loves me not', you know? And both sides are true. Or, neither side is true. The real truth, your heart's truth, is singular, and obvious."

"It's not obvious to me," Paco complained.

"Because you are not feeling deep enough in your heart, my friend. If you doubt, feel deeper. If you can't decide, feel deeper. Feel so deep, no thoughts move. Feel so deep, only openness shines. When you offer your life from this place of open depth, you act with absolute certainty, though you still might not have the slightest idea what you will do next. Without waivering, every action springs from love's depth."

Mykonos looked at Erin's anguished face.

"This depth of love is what Erin needs from you, Paco. Her mind is filled with doubts, too, so she might always seem confused about what she wants. She might always complain, even when you are not so ambiguous. All you can offer her is your absolute certainty of love, your depth of openness, now and now and now."

"I don't know if I love her."

"Feel deeper, then. Look into her eyes, feel the deepest part of her heart, and offer her the deepest part of yours. Do you want to embrace her?"

"Yes."

"Do you want to combine yourself with her sexually?"

"Yes."

"Do you want to have children with her?"

"No, not now, anyway."

"Do you want to live with her?"

"Yes."

"Will you still want to live with her tomorrow?"

"I don't know."

"EXACTLY!" Mykonos shouted. "You know nothing but the deep certainty of love, and how it wants to be expressed in this present moment. That is all you can ever know. Life lived spontaneously from your depth of love is a moment-to-moment gift. It is your art."

Mykonos paused to see if Paco understood. "My friend, when you live from your head, you are always caught in dilemmas. But when you live from your deep heart, life is singular because love is singular. Erin can feel your depth of heart, and trust you, day by day, as you offer your deepest truth to her. But when you are coming from the contradictions that fill your head, why should she trust you? She'd do better to chop your head off!"

"Sometimes I feel like chopping his head off," Erin admitted with a smile.

"Of course you do, ma. Unless Paco's mind is open like the sky, it's a box of complications, obstructing his love. Why not chop the damn thing off? Paco would be better off for it!"

"Yeah, I guess I would," Paco smiled.

"So, at depth, are you certain of your love for this woman, Paco?"

"Yes, Mykonos. I understand what you are saying. I can feel deeper than my doubt, but then I doubt that I will always be able to do it!"

"It's a moment-to-moment thing, Paco. Do it now. And now. It's a practice that grows over time, but the love itself, the openness itself, is deeper than time. Your mind and body are always struggling with contradictory thoughts and impulses. Feel deeper, open deep as love's certainty, and surrender your body and mind to be lived as love's depth, with Erin and everybody else. Erin, is there anything else you would want from Paco?"

"No. Of course not."

"Then that is it," Mykonos said. "Be lived as love, or be an asshole, Paco."

Remembering Mykonos's suggestions to Paco, I looked into Rebecca's eyes. Clearly, she felt my ambiguity. Part of me wouldn't let go of Gia. Part of me doubted that Rebecca—or any woman—could ever take Gia's place in my life. Part of me was afraid of hurting Gia. And part of me doubted that I was doing the right thing. Was I about to ruin Rebecca's life? Was I avoiding a deeper possible love with Gia by bringing Rebecca into the picture?

As I felt deeper than all of these thoughts and doubts in my mind, a certainty rose from my heart: it was time to change my relationship with Gia and begin one with

Rebecca. If I thought about it, though, then doubts would clench me and indecision would freeze me. But feeling deeper than thought, feeling into my deep heart, I was certain. I couldn't explain it, to myself or to anyone else, but I was certain that love was moving me to change relationships. I didn't know how it would turn out, and parts of me were still afraid, but, deep down, there was no doubt.

As soon as I felt the certainty deep in my heart, Rebecca shifted her posture. She stood taller and breathed more deeply. Her guardedness vanished.

"I love you," she said to me.

I felt Rebecca's heart open wide. My mind began comparing her with Gia. Is she as wise as Gia? Does she love me as much as Gia? I could see my mind's doubt reflected in Rebecca's eyes and body. When I doubted, Rebecca guarded her heart. When I felt deeper than doubt, when I opened my deepest heart and offered love's certainty to Rebecca, she opened, too. Her openness was my openness. There was no difference.

"All women are *she*," Mykonos once told me. "Treat each woman as the Goddess, because she is. Women are built to reveal openness—they are nature's mechanism of surrender—and they wait for a man they could trust with their utterly surrendered heart. Few women ever meet such a man, so most women suffer terribly, longing their entire lives."

I remembered Mykonos's words as I felt Rebecca responding to my depth or to my doubt, instantaneously. Her body was an exquisite reflection of how deeply open I was, moment by moment. Her relaxation, the look on her face, and the openness in her eyes were based on my depth. She was waiting, and as soon as I opened deeply and offered love's certainty, she surrendered open deeply—and her body opened to mine.

Opening as love with Gia, we shared unchecked affection, we shared our spiritual practice, we combined our talents to serve others. Gia and I shared subtle delights and life-changing insights with extraordinary ease. We could talk about anything—or simply exchange a glance or a touch—and understand each other in ways nobody else did.

Opening as love with Rebecca, our bodies were drawn together in sexual merger.

8
Being Claimed

∽

"I can feel Mykonos when we make love," Rebecca told me one day.

I was instantly offended. I wanted some credit for myself. After a few months of our lovemaking, Rebecca was opening to God through sex, and her life had changed profoundly. Her heart was able to feel what she called an "indescribable bliss" of "infinite being" for several days after we had been together. I had just spent time with Mykonos, and he had given me more instruction on sexual yoga. So I thought that's what she might be feeling.

"Maybe it's not Mykonos" Rebecca said, "but I can feel a certain energy when we make love that feels how I imagine Mykonos." She had never meet Mykonos. I had told her many stories of my time with Mykonos, but how could she know what he felt like? I wanted to claim my prowess as a divine lover, and now Mykonos was stealing my thunder.

One time, Mykonos and I were sitting in a small room in a house he once shared with his teacher, which Mykonos was caretaking. The energy of his teacher was tangible to me, like an unseen light pressing sweetly into my skin, pushing gently on my heart. Everything looked a little brighter, and the air seemed alive.

"Breathe it in," Mykonos told me. "Relax your body, open your heart, and breathe the force down your front." Mykonos had prepared me for this by teaching me how to breathe and stay open while very drunk, while exhausted in the middle of the night, while out in the cold ocean waves, and while making love. Compared to those circumstances, breathing his teacher's energy now felt easy and delicious, like drinking silky, radiant nectar.

"Soften your head and receive the energy down into your body. Relax your jaw and open your throat. Keep your mouth closed with your tongue pressed lightly against the roof of your mouth. Breathe the force down into you. Open to it like a woman opens to her lover. Let it press open your heart and into your belly. Breathe it down into your genitals. And when your belly and cock are full, let it rise up your spine as the light above. Then breathe it back down again."

Mykonos had taught me this practice many times before, but now something felt different. I was no longer breathing. The force was breathing me. I was being breathed. And the same living force that was breathing me was breathing everything. The same light that appeared as the house and landscape around us, the same energy that vibrated as sound and moved as thought, moved and breathed as me, as everything. The furniture, the room, the lawn outside, Mykonos, the air around us—everything altogether felt alive as the body of God.

"Yesss. To be a devotee of God means to be lived by the Great One. Some people are afraid to let go and be lived by the Great One. They are afraid of trusting the force of love. They are afraid of being possessed beyond their control. But they are already possessed, by their own ego, their own habits and patterns of fear. Why not allow yourself to be lived by love? Hmmm? Why not totally surrender to be lived by the Great One, the One alive as all, the One who appears even as this *room*?"

I let go and felt myself lived. All ownership and separation dissolved, and awakeness and light lived wide in the place of this moment. Yet, nothing made a difference. The light and force was intensely pleasurable, like the most perfect sex imaginable, pouring pleasure and love through my entire body—pouring through the entire world, which felt alive *as* my body. And it was all God. All infinite, magical, and yet totally empty, as if perfect sex and absolute indifference coincided. The pleasure of love's light was instantaneously absorbed in the depth of love's space, the nothingness of consciousness. A cosmic orgasm of bright infinity instantly evaporated in an even greater openness of being that never changed.

Love shone, and light dissolved in love. This was obviously always. Fully blissful, already gone, open as God's unchanging deep, alive as all. Mykonos was making occasional moaning sounds. I opened my eyes to look at him, and saw that he was transfigured in bliss, his crooked face warped in a spire of indescribable joy. His eyes were closed, so I closed mine.

"Do you see the light above?" he asked me.

"Yes," I answered.

"Breathe it down into your body. Down into your genitals."

I breathed the liquid light of love from infinite high down through a hollowness opening through my head and heart and belly and genitals. My whole body felt lit up and wide open, full and tumescent with love's force. My toes and fingers were splayed by the force of openness.

"When you fuck your lady, give her this," Mykonos said, "but don't forget the Great One who is living you.

And always remember, my friend," I opened my eyes to see Mykonos raising his hands as he spoke, "this place is such that she confers happiness by her own extinction. Her real nature is not perceived or known while she lives, but when she is embraced for the sake of the truth of her, she dies." Mykonos bowed slightly, extreme devotion shining through his face.

"What do you feel when we make love," I asked Rebecca, still stinging from her comment about feeling Mykonos when we had sex.

She smiled like I was an idiot for asking.

"Can you put it into words?" I wondered.

"No. I wouldn't want to."

"Could you try, for me?"

"Words can't touch it," she said. And then, with certainty, "It is death. Nothing. Everything. Infinity. God. Everything disappears, and it is so full. You kill me into God with your fuck. But it is not you as a person, really."

"What do you mean?"

"Well," she said, hesitantly, "I don't really even *like* you. I love you, though. You have opened me in ways I couldn't dream of. But as a person, I don't really like you that much. But I love your fuck. I love your cock. But, your cock is not you."

We remained silent for a few moments while I felt into what she was saying. Rebecca closed her eyes and seemed to go inward. She smiled, and with eyes closed she began speaking quietly.

"I am a slave to your cock, so perfect, vulnerable, and singular in mission. I am desperate for your love, penetration, and command. I long to be yours, surrendered to you, combined with you and completely claimed by your fuck."

Tears began to grow from the corners of her closed eyes.

"Your gentle kisses and tender beatings which have left me blissfully weeping are ever in my heart. My body, my cunt, my heart shutter at the thought of your sweetness having me, embracing me, seizing me...forever! I will always be your most willing and grateful prisoner, longing for your gift and dissolved by its bestowal. I love you."

I couldn't believe she was talking this way. Usually, Rebecca was closer to a mute than a poet. Now, her song of words thrilled my heart.

She opened her eyes and looked into mine. Her eyes endlessly deep, her heart open without limits. I let go and fell into her, opening with her, going open as unbound love alive as all.

And then I realized. She wasn't talking to me! She was talking to the Great One who was fucking her. She was talking to the force of love that fucked open the entirety of every moment—intensely during sex—the love that lived as us, the love that all died as. Looking into Rebecca's eyes, opening with her, I allowed myself to be lived by what was always alive as all. We were blissfully gone in the living force of love that had been made obvious in the house of Mykonos's teacher.

Rebecca smiled, and her sobbing became laughter. Once again, my claiming had been defeated open as love. I had achieved nothing. There was only God, and the less I needed to know of my own victory, the more love could show plain.

Plain love. Rebecca and I had no history together. We had sex and God, and that was it. She didn't even like me.

9
Two White Doves

Mykonos, Michelle, and I were sitting in chairs on a screened-in porch, enjoying the afternoon. Michelle and Dimitri had ended their relationship, and Michelle had come over to hang out.

"Hayseed was a poet," Mykonos said, referring to a soldier he knew who died in Vietnam. "He was a great man, capable of converting the most hellish circumstances into poetry."

Mykonos took a sip from his beer and continued speaking.

"One day we were walking through the jungle. We came upon two airmen—American pilots—hanging in the trees. They had been tortured, castrated, and their genitals had been shoved in their mouths."

I could hardly imagine such horror. Sitting with Mykonos having a beer, listening to the birds singing outside, the sun shining—life seemed so beautiful.

"It was a psychological war. They knew how to spook us. These airmen were displayed to freak us out, to frighten us."

Mykonos took another drink of beer.

"I remember looking at a letter that Hayseed was writing to his parents that evening. In it, he described coming upon 'two white doves lying dead in the grass.' You see, he couldn't describe what was really happening in the war to his parents. Two white doves. Hayseed was a poet in the most horrendous circumstances you can imagine."

Hayseed died in the war some weeks later, a few feet away from Mykonos, who was critically injured in the same attack.

"Most men are weak," Mykonos said to Michelle. "Most men are boys. They have not entered manhood. They do not know death."

"Mykonos," I said, "I've never seen death like you have."

"You are lucky. Pray you never have to. You don't need to go to war to be a man. That was my karma, my fate. You are lucky not to have to go through that kind of thing. Nobody should have to go through it. Few make it out alive.

And those that do, most come home insane. You can't live that way day after day and then come back home, get a job and get married and act like everything is fine. You've seen too much."

Michelle and I sat in silence, drinking when Mykonos drank, waiting to see where Mykonos wanted to go.

"Michelle, are you done with Dimitri? Is your relationship over now?" Mykonos asked.

"Yes. He wasn't the one for me."

"Why not?" Mykonos asked.

"I don't know. He wasn't strong enough, I guess."

"Dimitri is still a boy," Mykonos said. "He's a great guy. I love him. You both know I love him like a brother. But he still thinks it's all going to end up OK, you know? He believes that if he lives right, if he tries to be loving and social, then life is going to turn out all right. He's a love idealist. He hasn't tasted life yet, not really. He hasn't tasted life fully. This place is a horrible place."

"It's not that bad, Mykonos," Michelle said.

"One day, Michelle, your tits will hang like soggy pancakes and your ass will sag to your knees. You'll wake up in the morning, put your dentures in and paint your rotting face, and wonder which of your friends died today. The man who you finally find—if you ever find a good man—will probably have died long ago, or left you for a younger woman. You are going to die, Michelle, and it might not be so pretty. But we don't want to talk about that," Mykonos said with a faint smile, drinking his beer.

"But right now everything seems fine," Michelle said enthusiastically. "Why can't we enjoy things the way they are right now?"

"Michelle, what did you mean when you said Dimitri wasn't strong enough for you?" Mykonos asked.

"Well, it's hard to describe. He was nice to me. We had a lot of fun together. But…"

"But what?"

"Something was missing."

"What?"

"I don't know. He didn't really have a strong direction in his life."

"So, why don't you just marry a businessman?"

"I don't want to marry a businessman."

"Why not?"

"Because I want a man who is dedicated to God."

"'Dedicated to God,' huh?" Mykonos said smiling, as he took another chug of beer.

"Yeah, a man who is deeper than the average guy."

"And how would you know he was deeper?"

"I could just feel it."

"You mean you wouldn't want a guy who was a lot of fun to be with? A guy who enjoyed life with you?"

"Well, I want that, too."

"Michelle, what do you really want? I mean, *really*?" Mykonos questioned as he looked in Michelle's eyes.

"I want a man who could open me to God."

"And where is God?"

"Everywhere."

"Then what do you need a man for? Why do you want to be with a man if God is everywhere? Hmmm? Why can't you be happy right now?"

"I am happy."

"*Perfectly* happy?"

"No, not perfectly happy. But happy enough."

"Really?"

"OK. No. I'm happy, but not happy enough. Something is still missing."

"Exactly. Even when things seem OK, they are not perfectly OK. Even now, something is missing. You know it in your heart. One day, you will be too old to do much about it. You'll just ride out whatever is left of your dwindling life and try to make yourself comfortable as you slowly rot. But now, you are young and pretty, your cunt is wet and your face is still smooth. You look forward to getting laid, to finding a good man. That'll carry you through the day. But under it all, your heart is yearning. Hmmm? And even if you do find a good man, you will suffer and yearn for deeper love—unless you are surrendering your entire life to be lived open as love. Otherwise, as you try to cling to things turning out well, you are afraid, because you are dying, even now, and deep down, you know it."

"So, what am I supposed to do? Become a nun?" Michelle asked as she drank her beer and looked down at the floor.

"Women are beautiful, are they not?" Mykonos asked me, smiling.

"Yes," I said.

"Michelle," Mykonos said, "you're about as close to becoming a nun as you are to growing a cock. Your body is given to you. Enjoy it. Enjoy everything, all of life. This place can be a pleasure dome, a *room* where we can sing and dance and make love. This place is as good as any place—it's just dead, already. Right now."

Mykonos took a sip and held his beer high as if making a toast. "You have not seen it, unless you've seen your dead one there as silent as the mail."

Mykonos looked at Michelle. "If you let go of everything, what is left?"

Michelle closed her eyes for a moment. She breathed deeply and let go with a sigh. Then she opened her eyes again and smiled.

"Everything," Michelle said, beaming.

"What does your cunt feel?" Mykonos asked, seriously.

"Happy."

"Yes. Only when you let go completely can you truly live and open in love. You can only fuck for real when you are willing to let go of everything, even your body, and all bodies. You don't need to see dead soldiers hanging in trees to get that message. This place is about letting go. It is given to you for a time, and taken away. Nothing lasts. Nothing. Just ask Hayseed."

Mykonos stopped talking. His love for Hayseed was palpable. I felt a lump in my throat and swallowed.

"You want to be with a good man," Mykonos continued speaking to Michelle, "and that is fine. Why not? Why not enjoy these bodies, these relationships, this place of beauty? It is all God. But if you only feel the *room* you seem to be in, then you can't feel God in depth. You can only feel as deep as you feel."

Mykonos stroked his heart and looked at the horizon.

"The only way to get through a war without going insane is to know love, even as death surrounds you, as you wait to die yourself. And this moment is no different. Not really. It's a nicer picture, but everyone here is dying, and you can die in any moment. When you die, this whole place will fade and you will find yourself in another place, another *room*. It may seem like a nightmare or it may seem like a wet dream. It may seem like it does now. *Exactly as it does now.* In any case, you will be as riveted by others and events that seem to occur in that *room* as much as you are now."

Michelle was listening to Mykonos with total attention.

"Happiness is to sacrifice yourself to infinity, to always die wide open as love, holding onto nothing, giving yourself to everyone as if they were God, because they *are* God. Surrender as if you were dying right now, and find out what is left. Feel as deep and as wide as you can, until all you feel is feeling itself, and live open as feeling, alive as everyone and everything, no matter how horrible or beautiful the world seems."

"I can do that with or without a man, right?" Michelle asked.

"Definitely. You can do it with or without a body, ma! You can do it on the other side, after you die, when you are swirled in a clicking chaos of shifting shapes and nothing makes any sense. Surrender, love, openness is who you are. See everything as the light of God, now and after death. Treat everyone as God, be willing to dissolve in God if that's how it turns out—but always offer yourself as you are, right now, holding nothing back, alive as unbound openness. If you were to offer yourself to God now—if you were to give all of you to the Great One—how would your cunt feel?"

"Alive. Throbbing. I want to give myself to God through fuck," Michelle said, smiling wide and beaming.

"Yesss. Yes you do. You are not a tree. At least not for the moment," Mykonos smiled. "You are appearing in this *room* as a woman—a woman with a cunt that loves to be filled with God's fuck. Is it OK that I'm saying this?"

"Yes!" Michelle answered. "I've always felt this way. I've always been afraid to admit it. That's why I left Dimitri. He couldn't fuck me like I need it. I mean, we had good sex. He loved to lick my pussy, and he was a great kisser. He was really good to me. We had a fun time. But I want to be fucked to God. I want to be fucked *by* God. I want to be fucked…"

"…to death," Mykonos stated.

"Yes. I want to be fucked to death by God."

"Smithereened in love," Mykonos added, stroking his heart and smiling.

"Yes. Smithereened," Michelle agreed.

"And why not? What else would you rather do with your life, with your body, while it is still relatively young and healthy? When you are bent over with years, croaking on the shitter, you can give yourself to God as an old woman does, but for now, you want to give yourself like a cunt opening as big as the universe, hmmm? Is that what your heart wants?" Mykonos asked, tapping his finger on his heart.

"Yes. My heart wants to be fucked open to God."

"My friend," Mykonos said to me, "this is what everyone wants, one way or another. To see the horror of this place and not recoil, that is what it means to be a man. To stand strong in this knowledge of love, even when everything hurts, that is what it means to be free as a man. Hayseed was such a man."

Michelle was sitting up straight in her chair, breathing like a summer wind, her face radiant with love. Mykonos had fucked the entire moment open to God with his words, but his face also crevassed in sorrow as he spoke of his friend, Hayseed. And in my mind I saw two white doves lying dead in the grass.

10
Letting Go

～

We were sitting in a circle in the living room, on chairs and couches, masturbating.

"Layla, how much pleasure can that chubby body of yours handle?" Mykonos asked.

"What do you mean?" Layla wondered.

"I mean, my dear, can you feel God in your cunt?"

"I think so."

"Mm-hmm. Just as I thought," Mykonos grinned.

Mykonos, Lemuel, and I stroked our cocks while Layla rubbed her genitals.

"Clitoral orgasms are fine," Mykonos said, "but your cervix is where it's at, Layla. You know, you can touch yourself, or have your pussy licked, and there's nothing wrong with that. You can shiver your twat as much as you want.

But to be *really* fucked, your whole pussy has to open, like a surrendered heart, purring like a cat, swooning open in love, throbbing open beyond the moon's light as your heart is given over to God's fuck. Rubbing your clit isn't it."

"It feels good to me," Layla said.

"That's because feeling good is good enough for you, my little princess. Look at her," Mykonos said to Lemuel and me, "screwing up her face like she's about to get that rush of pleasure she wants so bad. Holding her breath and clamping down on her hoity energy, keeping it all locked up in that pretty little pussy of hers, building it up so she can do her thing. And when it's over, she'll still complain, you know what I mean, gentlemen?"

"I think Layla likes to complain," Lemuel said with a smile.

"All women like to complain," Mykonos laughed. "It's their way of foreplay. If you buy into it, the game never ceases. She criticizes you, you feel belittled and defend yourself, she criticizes you for being weak, and so on. You don't know how to treat a woman if you argue with her. She wants one thing, and one thing only, gentlemen. She wants to be fucked. There, have I said it? And I'm not talking about licking her clit, or putting your pecker in her and pumping a few times. I'm talking about fucking her to God, you know?"

"I don't think I've ever fucked a woman to God," Lemuel confessed.

"Lemuel, first you've got to learn how to leave Shaker Heights behind!"

"I haven't puked in a long time, Mykonos!"

"That's good. But it takes more than that. You've got to kill your father and fuck your mother, you know? You've got to leave your childhood behind and be a man. You've got some strange image of yourself—you're the underdog, your dick is too small, you don't think you're as good as your friends here. It's time to let all of that go, Lemuel. What do you feel when you stroke your cock?"

"Well, it feels good."

Mykonos smiled, shook his head, and looked down, grimacing in mock frustration.

"You and Layla, feeling good. Look, we all know that when you rub your clit or stroke your dick it feels good. Hmmm? That's not what *fuck* is about. That's not what we are here for—at least I hope not! Feeling good is for people who are afraid to feel God."

"I'm not afraid to feel God," Layla said, still rubbing between her legs.

Mykonos looked at her face and imitated her expression: a staid woman having some tea while doing needlework.

"C'mon, that's not what I look like," Layla said, annoyed.

"Layla, do you trust men?" Mykonos asked.

"Trust them for what?"

"To enter you."

"Well, some men."

"Who."

"Well, nobody right now. But I have trusted men."

"So you've totally received a man into your heart and body? Actively received him, worshipped his cock, sucked him into you so deep no part of you was unknown to his penetration? Hmmm? Have you opened yourself and taken him in so deep your heart is opened wider than the greatest love you have ever felt?"

"Well, I've opened to a man, but not that much."

"Mm-hmm. And why not?"

"Well, I'm afraid to lose myself."

"Yes, exactly. And that, my dear, is why your cunt is afraid of pleasure."

"My cunt isn't afraid of pleasure."

"Your clit isn't afraid, but your cunt is. When was the last time your cervix pulsed as wide as the universe, so that your body radiated as God's bliss in waves to infinity—so you lost yourself entirely, gone, I mean really gone, so great is the bliss of love's surrender?"

Letting Go

"How can my cunt be as big as the universe, Mykonos?"

"Layla, you have never been fucked."

"I want to be fucked," Layla said quietly as she stopped masturbating. She wiped her eyes with the back of her hand. Her whole body softened.

"I really do, Mykonos," Layla continued. "But I'm afraid. What happens if I give myself to a man and get hurt? How do I know he'll stay with me? I've worked a long time to trust myself, to not need a man to feel good about my life." Layla stopped talking and more tears welled in her eyes. "I know I've never really opened or given myself to a man completely. And now I'm afraid I'm getting old and I'll never find a man who I can trust."

"So, you're giving us a little Pi R Boo-hoo, are you? Your emotional geometry isn't going to work here, Layla. You might want your clit licked by a royal schmengie who bows at your painted toes, you might want to cry all comfy in the arms of your wealthy lover, but I'm not your boy, Layla. Look around this room. This isn't the place for you to find a daddy you can finally trust to do you like you always wanted. And this isn't Shaker Heights," Mykonos added, glancing over at Lemuel.

"This moment is as God as it gets, and it's the only home you'll ever have, the only beloved you will ever truly know, even in the form of your loyal, mustachioed lover, Layla. If you are looking for a better moment—or a better lover—you might as well sew that thing up right now," Mykonos said with a big smile, looking between Layla's legs.

"Daddy isn't just going to take care of you, he's going to obliterate you. Mommy isn't just going to feed you from her tit, she's going to eat you. The refuge you dream of is also the place of your crucifixion—right now, this very moment. Can you feel it? You want a man you can trust before you give yourself completely, Layla. So you are waiting, unblissful and unopen, before you will offer yourself to be claimed by God's fuck. But any man you ever meet is going to betray you. I guarantee it. Not because men are evil. But because this is a place of changes, and unless you are already submitting to the Great One's fuck—right now and in every moment—you will feel betrayed by change. Can you open your cunt now? Can you receive the force that obliterates you to the ends of time, the force that fills you as large as the universe spreads? Why do you think they call it the Big Bang, Layla? The force of the universe—the force of God—is the force of fuck. And this force, right now, is opening *as* you. Will you consent to open? Can you receive that force of opening so deep in your heart and body that your little fatty wagon vanishes in the perfect agony of love's bliss? Hmmm?"

Layla was rocking back and forth, touching herself again. She was breathing deeply and her body seemed soft and vulnerable. Her mouth opened and closed. She seemed about to have an orgasm, but instead of holding her breath and clamping down and squealing—as we had all seen her do before—she continued opening and breathing.

"Lemuel," Mykonos shouted, "breathe it down to your cock! Do not be afraid. Why are you hiding? Show us your face. Show us your cock. Show us your happiness. Allow your pleasure to be bigger than your fear. Hmmm? Can you feel your body, Lemuel?

"Yes."

"Who are you? Who is feeling the body?"

"I am."

"Yes, but who are you? What are you? Where are you, feeling your body?"

Lemuel closed his eyes and continued stroking his cock. Suddenly he smiled and opened his eyes.

"You are bigger than your pecker, aren't you Lemuel?" Mykonos asked.

"Yes."

"How big are you, hmmm? Feel as wide as you can feel, and tell me, how big are you, my friend?"

"Really big. I can't feel where I stop."

"Exactly, my friend. Your mommy and daddy aren't here with you, your pecker is disgusting, and you don't stop! Fuck as big as you can feel. Right now, open as fuck, holding nothing back!"

"I'm going to come!" Lemuel shouted.

"Shoot it up the spine, Lemuel. Breathe it down your front, breathe it back from your pecker and breathe it up your spine. Feel upward, Lemuel. Feel upward and let the energy go up."

"I can feel it going up," Lemuel said, his eyes turning upward so that the whites showed, his whole body vibrating.

"Good. Now don't forget who you are. Feel outward to infinity, even as the energy goes up. Let go of everything, even the pleasure. Open your heart as wide as you can feel. Feel as wide as God goes. Now open your eyes, Lemuel. Look at Layla."

Lemuel opened his eyes wide and looked into Layla's eyes. They were both masturbating furiously. Lemuel was still vibrating and Layla rocked back and forth, mouthing and mewling.

"Lemuel, feel into Layla's heart. All she wants is love. Give her all your love. Love this woman more than you've ever loved. Feel yourself fucking her open, feel into her, feel into her heart, opening her as wide as you can feel, wider than you are willing to feel, so wide you die open with her. Is your body vanishing, Lemuel?"

"It's getting hard to feel my body. Everything is all bright, all clear."

"Keep pumping your cock, Lemuel. Breathe the force down into your body, filling your belly and cock, and then let it rise up your spine, feeling into Layla all the while, fucking her open wider and wider with love's force. Let it all go. Let *everything* vanish as you give your love. Let your body go as you feel more pleasure than you've ever allowed. Layla, let it spread from your twat. Open your cunt up to your heart. Open your cunt bigger than your body."

"Yes," Layla sputtered, "yes, cunt, fuck, ah! Oh, God!"

"Open more," Mykonos said quietly. "Be willing to die open as bliss. Now is the only time. Don't just give or take fuck. *Be* fuck! Be open *as* fuck. Full as light, more life than you've ever allowed, blown open, taken to God, letting love open you, surrendering and letting the Great One fill you, open you, live you!"

Mykonos sat in silence for a while, stroking his genitals, and occasionally offering direction to Layla and Lemuel when they needed it. I continued masturbating, but the immensity of fullness far outshined any sense of my body's boundaries or pleasure.

"Now," Mykonos proceeded, "would you feel the same bliss if your body was being burned at the stake? Would you feel the same openness if you were being tortured? If your friends here were drowning before your eyes, and you could do nothing about it, could you feel the boundlessness of God? This moment is no different than any moment. Sex is useful because our bodies are built to surrender through sex. But it's not about sex. It's about the Great One, the love that lives as every moment, good and bad."

I wasn't sure that Lemuel and Layla were listening to Mykonos. They seemed lost in the froth of their own enjoyment.

"Right now, feel farther than your pleasure," Mykonos instructed. "Pleasure is fine. Pleasure is good. But one day, you may be feeling pain. One day, in fact, you may feel nothing—absolutely nothing. Could you open if you were feeling nothing, no body, no mind? Or would you clench if suddenly everything began to disappear? Imagine your body becoming cold and numb. Mind confused and fading. Everything becoming dark—and now nothing. Not a single thing. Are you ready for that? Or do you still need a boyfriend you can trust?" Mykonos laughed, looking at Layla.

Layla didn't answer.

Lemuel suddenly grunted, "I'm coming!"

Letting Go

"Show us your pleasure, Lemuel! There is nothing to hide. We *are* you! Feel outward to infinity! Open wider than this *room*! Orgasm as huge as the Big Bang!"

Lemuel opened his mouth and shouted as he came. Layla began sounding loudly, "Ohhh! Ohhh!"

"Soften your forehead, Layla," Mykonos said tenderly. "Soften your head and open your cunt as if you were receiving God's cock wider than the stars. Give yourself open to God, Layla! Die open in God's fuck like you've always wanted to!"

Layla began sobbing as she rocked back and forth, touching herself between her legs, tilting her head back, mouth opening, arching her spine, legs fluttering like a butterfly, mouthing unintelligible words, moaning, crying, shuddering in love's torment.

"What a place!" Mykonos said to me, talking quietly, allowing Layla and Lemuel their awesome pleasure. "Look at your friends here. They are so beautiful, so full of light. But imagine that you could see through their skin. Hmmm? What would you see? Blood, pus, and excrement. Bile, mucous, and urine. It's just a piece of meat, that cock or pussy you want so much. And if you could see it even more, down to the molecules and atoms, you would see mostly space, you know? Nothing here is worth clinging to—it's all just rotting meat, dancing electrons, and empty space—yet that is all most people do, cling to the withering flesh they have, and wait for something better to save them from the emptiness they dread.

"Everyone occupies their time while they wait for *the* big fuck, the thing they hope will finally make them happy, and all the while they are clamping down their pus-sack bodies, enjoying a few minutes of pleasurable dribble in an otherwise utterly boring day, holding back their hearts while they wait for a mommy or daddy who could save them and make them feel loved, denying God's fuck with the dumb, relentless churn of their doubting mind, resisting the Great One's love, the ever-present Big Bang of God's love exploding as everything they see and don't see, missing God appearing now while absorbing their terror in work and kids and whatever people do.

"Have I gone too far?" Mykonos asked.

"No, you haven't," I answered.

"Why can't you let go of Gia?" Mykonos suddenly asked me.

"I love her."

"I know you do. What else?"

I tried to feel into "what else." Rebecca and I shared an opening of love that felt endlessly deep, yet I still felt Gia in my heart. What was I feeling? Why did I feel Gia so often, wanting to talk with her every day, worrying about her when she was ill or dealing with some problem in her life? Why couldn't I let go?

"Mykonos," I said, doing my best to answer, "I just feel Gia is my dearest companion in life. I feel her in my heart all the time."

"Fine. Every man should love a woman before he dies. What else? Hmmm?"

I could actually feel Gia in the center of my heart, like a soft mass of familiar love.

"I'm comfortable with Gia. She is in my heart always. She feels like home."

"Yes. And you are afraid to leave home."

"I am afraid to leave Gia, to let go of her love."

"It's not her love you are afraid of letting go, my friend. It's the sense of home her love gives you. The familiar. It feels so good, knowing Gia will always love you, doesn't it?"

"Yes."

"She is completely devoted to you. She's not a cock worshipper like Michelle, but a truly one-man-devoted woman. And knowing she is at your side *forever* gives you comfort."

"Yes. She is always there for me."

"Oh, is she?" Mykonos asked.

"Well, almost always."

"She's not your mother. As good as her love feels, as warm as her love fills your heart, you are clinging to the tit and missing the moment's depth. You are afraid to be totally alone—that is, so open there is no other. NO OTHER!" Mykonos shouted. "You need an other so you can be assured of yourself. And the other you want—the one that gives you most assurance—is your mother. You want to feel her warmth, her smell, her support, her devotion to you—you won't let go of that."

"You're right. I'm holding on to Gia's love because I'm afraid to be alone without her," I admitted. "But sometimes I *do* open so fully there is no other. Even then, when I'm that open, it hurts to love Gia and let her go. My heart hurts feeling how much I love her."

"Yes, love hurts," Mykonos said. "You must learn to live wide open, hurting open with love. Not holding your love back—I've never told you to stop loving Gia—but always letting go of the false 'homes' you build out of fear. We are comfortable in our *rooms*. They protect us. They give us a sense of belonging and security—but they aren't real, and you know that."

"Yes," I said. "I do know that. But there are still lots of times when I'm afraid to let go of the most precious *room* in my life. And my heart still hurts with love. The other day I was looking into Rebecca's eyes. We were both wide open, loving each other without holding back. There was no other, as you say, only love loving love through two bodies. Her eyes were filling with tears. My heart was aching with love—if I were to love any more I would burst. Suddenly, I felt Gia in my heart. I'm opening with Rebecca as deeply as I've ever opened with Gia, and still I feel Gia in my heart! Rebecca felt like a stranger."

"You have been with Gia for what—fifteen years?" Mykonos asked. "It's natural for you to feel her in your heart. But what are you afraid of? Why won't you let go of the form of your relationship—of *all* form—while you continue to love Gia? And Rebecca? And everyone? Hmmm? Why isn't love sufficient? Why do you need to hold on to an other? Even while opening your heart beyond hold, loving so open it hurts, what are you afraid of?"

"I'm afraid to let go of a woman who loves me completely."

"That, my friend, is your problem."

Mykonos turned his head to look at Lemuel and Layla. Lemuel was lying back relaxing, his penis softening, a smile on his face. Layla had stopped touching herself, but she was still moving her legs together and apart, her eyes closed.

"Our beautiful friends here, they are each in their *rooms*. Infinity surrounds them—*is* them—and yet they prefer to attend to their personal cocoons of sensual and emotional pleasure. That's how it is when things feel good—you want to oink into the feeling of goodness like a pig. You like the *room* you share with Gia, and you are afraid of losing it, because you need an other to comfort you, a place, a familiar mind and body and feeling of relationship. You can soothe your suffering—your terror of death, of infinite chaos, of no thing—while you groove on an orgasm, or on that warm feeling in your heart you get when you think of Gia. But it's not going to last, and your entire need to feel an other—even lovingly—is always riding on that fear."

"But that doesn't mean I shouldn't love Gia."

"Of course not. Open inside the *room* and outside the *room* at the same time, my friend. Love Gia with all of your heart. Feel your heart ache as you open to love her even more. And also feel how you cling to the sense of an other—mommy, the goodness of her love, the warmth of her, your sense of being at home with her. You cling to an other—and especially to the comfort and assurance of an other's love—because you are afraid of death. And that is what limits you. Love Gia completely, and let her go. Love Rebecca completely, and let her go. Love everyone, every moment, fully, achingly, and let it all go. Let go so you don't even know where you are, so all *rooms* of familiarity have slithered away in the fullness of love's bright release. There is nothing, absolutely no thing!"

"I can feel my fear of total nothingness."

Letting Go

"Yes. And that is why you are afraid to let go of Gia, and why Rebecca's love doesn't feel the same. Rebecca's love—even when it is full—doesn't have the familiar flavor, the smells of home, the fresh baked bread, the support that Gia has always given you. Rebecca doesn't feel like home—yet. Her love still opens as the ungraspable, unknowable fullness of no thing. So you miss Gia's familiar textures. You miss mommy. You miss the home you know."

Mykonos sat silently for a few moments, watching Layla and Lemuel relax in their pleasure.

"There comes a time when you've got to fuck your best friend in the ass and say goodbye," Mykonos said, looking at Lemuel.

I had known Lemuel even longer than I'd known Gia. If there was one person in the world who I felt more at home with than Gia, it was Lemuel.

"I'm not saying you shouldn't love," Mykonos continued. "I'm not saying that at all. Your love for Gia and Lemuel is beautiful. But you are holding onto the love you know, and you are unwilling to trust the love that is unknown, that can never be known. You are afraid to leave home, my friend, with no ground beneath you and no *room* to shelter you. You are afraid to die open with no form. No praise or blame. Everyone is afraid. At some point, though, whenever you are ready, you will have to pass through that absolute terror.

Knowing nothing. No thing. Nada. Dying completely, and finding out what, if anything, continues. To love completely and hold onto nothing—that is the only freedom."

I remembered lying in bed and snuggling with Gia. Laughing with her so many times over so many years. Opening with her and sharing our deepest secrets, our fears, our real dreams. We gave each other our lives. Together we stepped into the world and offered our gifts. I wasn't ready to let go of that, completely. I wanted to feel the possibility of it continuing, knowing Gia was with me, or at least waiting for me.

"Layla," Mykonos asked, "what would you do if suddenly you found yourself without a body?"

"I'd be the light of the moon," Layla answered.

"Yes, I believe you would," Mykonos laughed.

11
Big Waves

Mykonos suggested that we go surfing. We grabbed our boards from behind the house and headed to the beach. When we got to the ocean, the waves were huge. Way too big to surf. A storm was coming in, the wind was blowing hard and cold, the sky was gray with dense clouds, and the water was wild. Not a single person was on the beach or in the water. We stood on the sand and looked out at the churning water. An incessant wall of monster waves continually crashed as the wind howled.

"Well, are you ready to go out?" Mykonos asked.

Surprised, I wondered why Mykonos wanted to go out in these conditions. Even the big time surfers weren't out. These waves weren't just extremely large, they were messy, closing out, crashing down in a violent churn instead of providing smooth conditions for surfing.

"It looks pretty rough," I said, afraid that Mykonos would still want to go out. The wind began to blow even harder and colder. Sand whipped up from the beach, stinging my skin and eyes. Through half-closed eyelids, the water looked very harsh and menacing.

"Well, I don't know about you, but I'm going out," Mykonos said, walking into the water, and paddling out.

I was afraid. Mykonos was bringing me to the edge of my fear, as he often did, but I also wondered whether going out in these waves was just plain stupid. Our lives would definitely be at risk, and the conditions were so chaotic that the surfing wouldn't be enjoyable. I doubted we would be able to ride a single wave—and if we did, the probability was high that a forty-foot wall of impending water wouldn't provide us with surf, but would come crashing down on us, burying us deep below the furious surface, churning us down and around in the current's suction.

Mykonos was a vet—sometimes I wondered if he required the adrenaline rush of near death encounters to feed some kind of need. I didn't know if this situation was a spiritual test of my courage, or just Mykonos being self-destructive.

I followed Mykonos into the water.

I had decided years before that I would go wherever Mykonos led me. Other than his teacher, Mykonos was the most open, deep, and fearless person I had ever met. And always his direction had led me deeper and more open in love—so far.

From the beginning, his boundary-free love revealed my fear. When we would drink beer or sake, Mykonos would continue drinking far beyond my limit. At first, I stopped when I felt that I was getting too drunk. I noticed that Mykonos would stop then, too—in fact the evening would stop. So, I learned to match Mykonos, drink for drink, and go where Mykonos took the evening. I let go of my own fear—I listened to my inner voice of self-preservation, but I did not choose to obey it—and in doing so I discovered a wondrous expanse of beauty and love that lay outside my fearful perimeters.

Once, we were sitting in a room with four other people. We had been drinking for hours. I practiced, as Mykonos had taught me, breathing while feeling the open moment without clinging to or resisting anything. Mykonos was drinking hard and talking fast—everybody else had either passed out or was too fuzzed to follow the conversation.

"There is nothing," Mykonos said. And that is what I felt. Nothing. Absolute absence. "Yet everything appears," he continued. I saw the room, heard his voice, felt my own drunken state—and yet it was also nothing, as if a dream were being constantly evaporated, instantly, always, too soon to do anything about, and yet the images appeared, materialized, vanished. "Love is the only way to live that is not insane," he said.

"Love. Love. Love. Love…." Mykonos kept repeating that word, over and over, until it was just a sound. "What does it mean, 'love'?" Mykonos asked. "Love. Love. Love…" Hearing Mykonos repeat "love," there was no meaning to the utterance; it was just a sound, a shape.

"You do not know what a single thing is," Mykonos said. "Everything is happening. We can talk about it. But still, nothing means anything when you fully feel it in the present. You can associate a meaning with it—whatever 'meaning' means—but you do not know what it is. It simply is."

I looked around the room at the unconscious or nodding-off people. Mykonos was wide awake, sitting on the edge of his chair, passionately speaking.

"Everything is just…happening. That is the most that can be said. You can construct all kinds of words and thoughts and ideas—shapes in the mind—and associate them with the shapes you see—the glass of water, your friends here, the grass outside—but that doesn't mean you know what anything is. You have simply associated various shapes together. Patterns patterning. You can feel, even now, that those patterns are nothing, can you not?"

"Yes, Mykonos, everything feels like nothing."

"Everything *is* nothing. And yet it all exists. What a miracle! How can you live in such a place without going insane, unless you love? Hmmm? Your closest friends are shapes, coming and going, meaning nothing before this birth or after death, yet occupying your life with patterns of bodies and filling your heart with patterns of feeling."

Mykonos looked out the window, paused for a while, and continued speaking.

"Your heart would be crushed in suffering if you could actually feel all the beings in pain, the cats and dogs, men at war, women at home, lonely and unloved, all the children starving, dying, the disease—but here we are, enjoying ourselves, because we are able to limit our attention to the shapes in our little *room*, and act like we know what this is, what everything is."

Mykonos drank, and I drank. Then he looked in my eyes with such love, speaking intensely, but quietly.

"You are wide open. This *room* is wide open. God is alive as everything that appears and disappears, you included. You are either seizing up in fear—binding yourself to what appears, friends, lovers, children, homes, work, your body, your thoughts, building up a sense of self, a whole inner world of comfort and ideas and hopes for the future and so forth—or you are surrendering it all, loving *completely* and letting go *completely*. Love without limits, my friend. Trust love to live you and all things. As much as it hurts your heart to feel everything and everyone, as terrifying as it is to surrender absolutely, your only real option is to love without boundaries, wide open. Love is the only way to live. Feel everything. Feel without limitation."

I was drunk, and yet Mykonos's words rang crystal clear, opening my heart beyond hold. Why not open and love? I felt nauseous, dizzy, about to pass out—but why not love? Why would I want to collapse my feeling less than love? I breathed and relaxed my body, as best I could. I felt my body, the air in the room, and everybody in the room with us. I felt Mykonos's passion, the pain etched in his face, the light in his eyes, his constant efforts to bring me open—to bring everyone into love. My heart felt like it was turning inside out in gratitude.

"Do you know how many people have died?" Mykonos asked. "And every one of them was trying to survive, to feel good, to avoid too much pain, if possible. Some made grand gestures, and vestiges of their lives surround us as art, religion, science, whatever. Most made smaller gestures: a few kids, a comfortable living room, friends they could talk with as the patterns of their lives came and went."

Mykonos and I drank.

"And then there are the rare ones," said Mykonos, eyes glistening, "like my teacher, who appear in the pattern to remind the pattern itself of its source and true nature. I have been reminded, and you have been reminded, and until the whole pattern realizes that it is only love—*only love*—war continues here, pattern against pattern, each trying to carve out a little place of comfort, brushing up against other patterns trying to persist as they are, fighting against all that threatens them, forgetting love even as they fight with their lovers, their children, their own impulses—fighting with the very patterns they hope will save them.

"Alcohol can be useful if you know how to use it. It can help you see the patterns for what they are by softening the torrent of your jabbering mind-current. But most people just get dull when they drink. They don't know how to breathe life through their body, so, instead, the spirit-force backs up—rather than sinking down, opening their heart, and filling their belly with love's force, it rises up their front and makes them puke. Most people don't know who they are when their mind stops, so they feel confused, lost, or they just blank out when no thought moves, when their thinking mind is obliterated. They can't stand the gap. But if you can relax as love, if you are comfortable with no-thought, if you can simply be consciousness without needing a self-sense to cling to, then drugs and alcohol can help sweep away the usual and incessant patterns of body and mind so you can recognize love now—your mind, every body, this entire universe, is only love, appearing as patterns, and it all comes and goes, and surrender is the only way to live that isn't terror, you know?"

Paddling out into the churning sea, I tried to surrender rather than freeze up in terror. Mykonos was ahead of me, ducking under waves as they came in, paddling further out. The waves were much bigger now than they had seemed from the shore. I genuinely felt we might die. We were idiots. There wasn't a soul anywhere on the beach or in the water, the sky was darkening with storm's gray, and the waves kept getting bigger. We paddled outside of the area where the waves were breaking. This far from the shore, the swells were huge, lifting us up and down like tiny floating specks. As I looked back toward the beach, I could see the waves breaking, careening toward shore, monster walls of roiling, crashing madness.

Mykonos's face looked serious. The air was turning chillier as the winds whipped faster. Spray from the chop whacked our faces and filled our nose and eyes. The waves were now so large I didn't think we could make it back in. I paddled toward Mykonos. I assumed he had a plan.

"This was a pretty stupid thing to do," Mykonos said without smiling. I heard him quietly say his teacher's name, three times.

We stayed for more than an hour rising up and down with the swells outside of the break, waiting for the storm to subside, but it was only getting worse. On the shore, through the gray mist and white spray, we could see what I thought was a coast guard vehicle pulling up on the beach. They were yelling something through a megaphone, but we couldn't make out what they were saying over the roar of the crashing waves.

There was nothing we could do. I had followed Mykonos into this situation, willingly. I couldn't blame him.

Suddenly, Mykonos said, "I'm taking this one in." He paddled to catch the next wave and disappeared. All I could see was the back of the wave, charging into shore, until the wave broke into whitewater. I strained my eyes to find Mykonos, but I couldn't see him.

I was alone on the swells. Mykonos was gone. The evening's looming dark was adding to the visibility problems. I could barely make out the shore through the darkness. And then I saw Mykonos, a tiny speck carrying his board, walking toward the coast guard people. He had made it.

I felt the swells as I tried to calculate which wave to take in, but I was too afraid. I didn't know what to do. I tried paddling parallel to the shore, thinking that maybe I would find a place where the waves weren't breaking so hard, where I might be able to ride a wave all the way to shore without being crushed beneath its furious load. I realized it was getting late and soon I wouldn't be able to see a wave's gray shape looming against the night sky.

I was alone. Mykonos was safe on shore. The coast guard could do nothing.

There was no option but to take a wave in, and pray. I paddled back and forth for another twenty minutes or so, alternating between moments of strange peace and mind-numbing panic. I didn't know what I was waiting for—the conditions were only worsening. Finally, I forced myself to take a wave, and I held onto my board as I was lifted up and then dropped over a charging ledge into dark space.

Once, when drinking with Mykonos and our friends, Erin disappeared. We all looked for her in the house, and then we looked outside in the yard. Nobody could find her. As dawn approached, someone found her a few blocks from the house, lying on the side of the road, naked, passed out. She seemed fine, although she couldn't remember what happened to her.

During another drunken evening, a friend's wife disappeared with another man. She ended up divorcing my friend, marrying the other man, giving birth to a seriously handicapped child, divorcing her new husband, and years later, regretting that she ever spent time with us at all.

I trusted Mykonos more than anyone I had ever known—and he was also the least trustable person I knew. He frequently told me what a jerk someone was—and then acted like he was that person's best friend when they showed up. He lied and made up stories and twisted facts to suit the needs of the moment. He would pour his life into helping someone for years, and then never speak to them again, for no reason at all.

He was more loving, more compassionate, than anyone I had ever met, and he also couldn't care less about anyone's life. Nothing about my—or anyone's—daily life interested him. Months could go by and Mykonos would never ask a single question about how I was doing or what was going on in my life. Except for a few rare moments over the course of many years, he didn't want to hear about my relationships, my career, or even my health. He'd listen for a few seconds and then change the subject—always to sex or death or God, which were all the same thing to him. He would talk for hours about his time in Vietnam or his childhood friends, and later I would realize I didn't know anything more about Mykonos than before, but I had learned a great deal about love and how to open as love, and about death.

I heard people talk about Mykonos. A few people respected Mykonos greatly. But many more hated him. They told me he was a "back stabber," how he had pretended to be their friend only to shaft them later. They told me how he would never admit to being wrong, and that he would never talk about his own spiritual or sexual issues.

With other people, I saw Mykonos say one thing to their face and tell a totally different story when that person wasn't present, so I figured he did the same with me. One time, he strongly insisted that Paco prepare himself for an upcoming disaster, and then later he joked with me about how Paco was so neurotically insistent about preparing himself for the disaster. This kind of two-faced behavior was so common for Mykonos that I simply assumed he told every person a different story, perhaps what he felt they needed to hear, with no concern for what the facts "really" were.

Mykonos had no friends—at least not the kind of friends most people have. I had known Lemuel since childhood. Paco and Dimitri had been close friends of mine for many years. We shared a sense of loyalty. I knew I could count on them for the long haul. But unless I called Mykonos on the phone, or went to visit him, he never would even contact me. And, as far as I could tell, he was this way with just about everyone.

And yet, nobody gave me more than Mykonos. I couldn't count on him to help me in bad times, or even to call me in good times. I couldn't trust a word he said about anything. I assumed he criticized me in front of others just as he criticized them to me. And I knew, if I didn't get in touch with him, I'd never see him again—he'd never seek out my company, or anyone else's.

Still, the gifts that poured from Mykonos in an hour of drinking beer with him left me stunned, opened, grateful, and awakened to a dimension of heart-truth that my other friends—the friends I trusted with my life—barely knew existed.

Mykonos wasn't a person, really. He was a hole in the universe.

The wave began crashing down on me. I closed my eyes as the water pounded my body. I gripped the board as hard as I could, knowing that if I lost the board, I would be dragged beneath the water by the churning force of the wave, unable to come up for air. I was being washing-machined, sucked down and tumbled in the water. In the darkness, I couldn't tell what was up or down. I held to the board with all my strength, holding my breath, tumbling head over heels, waiting for the buoyancy of the board to bring me back to the surface before I began breathing water into my lungs.

I could feel my heart beating. The roar from beneath the water sounded like distant drums. I was running out of breath, out of time. I began to suffocate. There was nothing else I could do but wait for the board to bring me to surface. I waited, searing in my head and lungs.

When I hit the surface, I gasped for breath and inhaled ocean spray. Choking, another wave came down, burying me beneath the water, tumbling me upside down and around in the darkness. I reached again the surface and tried to breathe, coughing up water while clinging to the board. The next wave was smaller, pushing me closer to the shore that I could barely see through the spray. Regaining enough breath, I paddled and kicked to help the waves push me toward the beach.

Finally, I got close enough to the shore to see it clearly, although I couldn't see Mykonos or the coast guard people. Paddling through the chop and currents, I reached the shore, got out of the water on weary legs, and sat on the sand, my heart pounding hard.

I had drifted about half a mile from where Mykonos and I entered the water. After a few minutes, I walked back, chilled, feeling very good to be on land.

Mykonos was sitting on the beach looking out at the water when I reached him.

"Where did the coast guard people go?" I asked.

"They left a little while ago. You hungry?" Mykonos asked.

We went to a little Mexican food place near the beach. Mykonos never again mentioned our day in the stormy waves.

12
Cats and Dogs

"Look into her eyes," Mykonos suggested. We were on the grassy property surrounding the house Mykonos was caretaking for his teacher, standing outside the cage of two large monkeys. One of the monkeys was staring right at me.

"That's the girl," Mykonos said, explaining that the two monkeys were a mother and a daughter. "They are pretty aware monkeys."

I did feel like I was being *seen*, somehow, by this monkey looking into my eyes. Mykonos was cleaning out the cage, which was huge—the size of a small house filled with small trees, bushes, and even three chairs. The girl monkey and I held our gaze for several minutes before she decided to move to another branch and munch on a leaf.

"My teacher sometimes sits in one of those chairs," Mykonos pointed out, "and the two monkeys sit in the others. It's amazing. They spend hours together, the three of them, just sitting and looking at each other. I think my teacher prefers the company of some non-human beings more than he does some humans."

"Does he think animals can be as spiritually aware as humans?" I asked.

"In a way. It's like with humans. There are dense people and more open, aware people. Well, there are cats that are just cats, and then there are cats that are more in tune with the Great One than some humans are. Of course, non-humans don't have the language to talk about it, but so what? They commune with the Great One through different means than humans."

"What about dogs?" I wondered.

"Most dogs have been too domesticated over hundreds of years. They have been bred to obey. They aren't free enough to feel much beyond their lives of obedience and reward. Some dogs can break free, but not most. Cats, on the other hand, are less domesticated, freer in their feeling. Less manageable. Try teaching a cat to fetch a stick, or to sit when you tell them to. Cats are too free in their feeling to obey like a dog."

Before I ever met Mykonos face to face, I had heard about him. I had been getting to know some of the students of Mykonos's teacher. They told me that Mykonos had been kicked out of their spiritual school—by his teacher. When I asked them why his teacher had kicked Mykonos out, they told me that Mykonos had disobeyed him by refusing to teach in public. Because Mykonos refused, his teacher kicked him out, and then told the entire community of students to shun Mykonos—not to speak with Mykonos or interact with him in any way.

Then, over the next few months, I heard more stories about Mykonos, who had been ousted by the teacher he gave his life to for almost 20 years. Mykonos was now living with his wife in a friend's suburban house. A few students tried to speak with Mykonos and convince him to obey his teacher. Mykonos apparently chased them away with a baseball bat. I heard another story about Mykonos punching one of the students who tried to physically drag him to a meeting with the other men of the school.

These stories intrigued me. I had been studying and practicing with various spiritual teachers since I was a teenager, but I had never heard anything like this before. Everyone who I talked with agreed that Mykonos was the most advanced student in their community, yet now he seemed hated for disobeying his teacher.

I got Mykonos's phone number from one of the students who was still his friend and wrote it down on a little piece of yellow paper. I held onto that phone number for days, sometimes taking it out of my pocket, looking at it, and putting it back, afraid to call this man who chased people with baseball bats and beat them up, this man who was, I presumed, far more spiritually advanced than I was, yet kicked out by his own teacher for disobedience and shunned by the community of his peers. I knew he had spent the last twenty years meditating, doing spiritual exercises, and living in his teacher's company. I had to meet this man, but I was waiting for the right time to call.

One day, I was standing outside a building waiting for Gia to finish shopping. I saw a payphone, put a few coins in, took the piece of paper from my pocket, and dialed the number.

"Hello?" the voice answered.

"Hello, I'm trying to reach Mykonos," I said.

"This is Mykonos."

"Hi. I've been speaking to some of your friends, and, well, I feel I have to meet you."

"OK. Come on over," Mykonos said, and gave me directions to his house.

I dropped Gia off at home and drove to the house where Mykonos was staying. I stood in front of the door, ready to knock, not knowing what to expect. I thought Mykonos might wear robes of some kind, or he might look like a saint, downtrodden, rejected by God. Or maybe he would attack me like he had the others who tried to speak to him.

I knocked on the door, and a woman opened it.

"Hi," I said, "I'm here to see Mykonos."

"Come on in," she said, motioning me toward the living room.

I walked into the living room. A football game was on the TV. Mykonos was sitting on the carpet, cross-legged, somewhat hunched over, wearing a T-shirt and shorts, staring at the TV.

I didn't know if I should disrupt Mykonos—I was pretty sure it *was* Mykonos—while he was watching TV, or if I should wait until he looked over at me.

I stood and waited.

Finally, when he didn't do anything, I said, "Hi."

"Hi," Mykonos answered, his eyes still on the football game. "I'll be with you in a second."

I stood in the living room, watching Mykonos watch TV. When the game was interrupted by the next commercial break, Mykonos stood up. He opened the sliding glass door that led to the back yard, and he walked outside. He did not close the door behind him, so I followed him out, and slid the door closed.

Mykonos sat down on the bench of a picnic table set up in the back yard. I sat down across from him. He still didn't look at me. He gazed out over the small pond that divided the yard from the neighbor's.

"I don't really know why I'm here," I said, needing to say something to break the silence. "I've heard stories about you and your teacher, and I'm trying to understand. How can you trust a teacher and yet go against him—if that's what you did?"

I waited for an answer. Mykonos didn't move.

Finally, he turned from the pond and looked directly in my eyes. It was the first time I felt Mykonos's peculiar gaze, piercingly deep. His eyes were a bottomless well of open blackness. His nose was clearly crooked to one side, like it had been broken and healed off-center. His hair was long, scraggly, and unkempt. His shoulders were somewhat hunched, his limbs wiry, and yet the overall impression was one of intense strength—he could have been a hired killer.

Mykonos looked into my eyes for a few seconds. His face looked so serious.

Then he looked back over the pond, and spoke.

"What do you want to know?"

I felt like my entire life had led to this moment, and this question. My body was trembling slightly, but deep inside I felt calm and clear.

"I've heard you are the most advanced student of your teacher," I said.

I waited a few seconds to see how Mykonos would respond. He didn't move or change his expression at all.

So, I continued. "I'm not exactly sure why I called you, but I felt you had something to teach me—and I wanted to know what really happened to you, how you ended up here."

Mykonos smiled very slightly, still looking over the pond.

"What did you hear?" Mykonos asked.

"I heard that your teacher asked you to teach in public, and you refused. So you were kicked out by your teacher, who instructed the rest of his students to shun you."

Mykonos didn't respond, so I continued.

"I also heard that you threatened to hit some of his students with a baseball bat when they came to visit you," I added.

"Assholes," Mykonos said quietly, looking over the pond.

I waited without speaking. I didn't really have anything else to ask. If Mykonos wanted to say something, I was eager to listen. But if he didn't, then that was his choice.

A woman—not the one who had answered the door—appeared with some iced tea. By the way she and Mykonos exchanged glances, I assumed she was Mykonos's wife.

"Hi," she said to me, placing the tall glasses of tea down on the picnic table, making eye contact with Mykonos again before walking away. She wore more make-up than I expected to see on someone who was supposed to be a spiritual practitioner. Most people thought Mykonos's wife was at least as spiritually advanced as he was—but to my eyes, in that moment, she looked too dressed up and Mykonos too hunched over.

Mykonos took a sip of tea, put the glass down, and looked into my eyes.

"There are a lot of assholes out there," he said. "I'm just lying low, doing some writing."

Mykonos glanced toward some books that were stacked on the picnic table. Spiritual texts, mostly imported from India. Then he looked again over the pond.

"Did your teacher ask you to start speaking in public?" I asked Mykonos, trying to get the conversation to go somewhere. "I heard that he wanted you to be the head of some branch of your school, and you refused."

"I'm not about to be the head of anything," Mykonos said.

"But I thought that if you trust a teacher, you're supposed to obey him," I said, hoping that Mykonos would clarify this for me.

Mykonos drew back his lips and exposed his front teeth for a few seconds, looking like a mean beaver about to bite into wood.

"Years ago," Mykonos said, "my teacher told me that one day he would have to kick me out, send me out into the world, and all I would have with me is this orange book." Mykonos nodded toward a small book with an orange cover that was sitting on the table, separate from the other books.

"So you knew this was going to happen?" I wondered aloud.

"I didn't know anything then, and I don't know anything now," Mykonos said, "but here I am."

I started to feel that he was avoiding my questions. Then he looked into my eyes and I felt the endless black openness.

Holding my gaze, Mykonos spoke.

"There is obedience, and then there is *obedience*. Those assholes don't have the slightest idea what's going on. It's not like the teacher tells you what to do, and then you're supposed to do it. It's not like that at all. It's all a play, a test. I'm not about to fucking become an institutional-type."

"But your teacher said that you should head up some kind of institution, didn't he?" I asked Mykonos.

"Yes. He's said lots of things," Mykonos told me and looked over the pond without saying anything more.

I really wanted to understand this. I was at a point in my life where I realized I needed a teacher to help me take the next step, and yet most people I saw who had spiritual teachers did, in fact, seem like assholes. Mykonos knew something deeper, I felt.

"Mykonos, I don't mean to be rude…" I said, and Mykonos turned his horse-like head straight toward me.

"I need to know what you know," I told him.

"Why?" Mykonos asked.

"You know why," I answered, shocked by my own brusqueness.

"Yesss," Mykonos said, smiling, "perhaps I do. Are you willing to give up everything? Because that's what it takes. My teacher, he's taken *everything* from me. I've got this orange book, and that's it. He's taken my wife, my daughter, my life. I have nothing. He's even kicked me out so I can't live with him," Mykonos smiled. "It's a beautiful thing."

"So, you don't mind being kicked out?" I asked.

"This? It's nothing. You have no idea, my friend."

We continued talking for a few hours before I said goodbye, shaking Mykonos's hand, thanking him, and leaving. In those few hours, Mykonos somehow imparted—more through his disposition than his words—what it means to be an authentic student. My heart was opened to a depth of love—an actual and tangible depth of reality—that I had never felt before. This depth had always been present, but I had been more attentive to the surface of things, what people said and did, the events in my life.

Sitting with Mykonos in that backyard, a depth unperturbed by time swelled into my feeling, and it became obvious how Mykonos could seemingly disobey his teacher, and yet remain *obedient* at a level that most people couldn't even perceive. As he told me, on the surface, it looked like he and his teacher were at war. But the war was always already over, and love had won, even if the fight continued to appear on the surface.

After my meeting with him, Mykonos remained apart from his teacher for three years, and then he was, once again, closer to his teacher than any other man. It was as if the separation had never occurred. In Mykonos's heart, it hadn't. In the years that I subsequently spent with Mykonos, he disobeyed his teacher all the time. Eventually, as I observed their "battle" more and more, their tussling came to feel like a chess match between two close friends more than an actual fight. And yet, underneath all the scheming and apparent disagreements, a huge oneness of love prevailed. This immense being, this open force of love-bliss, emerged through whatever seemed to be happening, and communicated itself regardless of what Mykonos was saying or doing.

"Cats are, in general, less domesticated than dogs. But then there are the silverback gorillas," Mykonos continued speaking as he cleaned around the monkey cage. "The silverbacks know they are facing extinction. There are only a few of them left. My teacher said he'd much rather spend time with the silverbacks than with most people that come to him. He's spent a lot of time with these monkeys here," Mykonos said, nodding his head toward the mother and daughter who were now grooming each other. "If you look into their eyes, you can feel the same love-bliss you feel around my teacher. These two monkeys are more in touch with where it's at than most humans."

"Mykonos, do you really think that monkeys are as evolved as humans?"

"Well, they don't have the same kind of thinking mind as humans. They don't speak like humans, but then, they don't need to. Humans are unique in their capacity to reflect upon themselves—which is why we are so into sex and death. We think about our own life all the time, wondering when we will finally be fucked like we've always been waiting for—and you know what I mean by 'fuck'. Humans are also aware of their impending death, so they begin to wonder about the meaning of their life. Most non-human beings don't think about fuck or death. So they don't build culture like humans."

Mykonos looked at the monkeys as he continued speaking.

"They don't need monuments or books to help them reflect themselves to themselves, like human do, like human thought does. Of course, they don't have the capacity for self-understanding that humans do, either. To be born human is to be born with a capacity to transcend what appears through self-understanding—non-human beings haven't developed that capacity. But then, most people haven't, either. Compared to these monkeys here, most people are self-enclosed assholes, don't you think?"

I looked into the mother's eyes. She looked right back at me, relaxing, chewing on a leaf. She jumped to a closer branch, checking me out. Looking into her unflinching gaze, I felt her depth of consciousness, a feeling of alert and gentle openness.

Mykonos finished cleaning around the cage. He stood up—as straight as Mykonos ever stands—and gazed out over the grassy landscape. My mind stopped. The birds and crickets chirped. Occasionally the monkeys would jump to another branch. The wind was warm, and now and then the leaves would rustle in the breeze.

"I'm leaving soon," Mykonos said. "I'm not sure exactly when, but I'm going to see my teacher."

I knew Mykonos's teacher was currently residing outside of the country, but I didn't know Mykonos was planning to leave.

My mind began to move again, imagining Mykonos gone. But then the ripples of thought subsided, and we stood in silence. The quietness felt like soft wool pressing down, muffling the vibrations of the world. I could still hear, but sounds seemed so distant. I could still see, but the landscape seemed translucent and thin, as if silent light were shining through a space barely occupied by tickles of form.

The silent light felt emergent from my heart, but even my body dissolved in the invisible fullness.

"Non-human beings are of the same One," Mykonos said, "but humans can develop the capacity to live entirely free as that One, open beyond the tendencies and patterns that seem to move in this place. But you've got to practice feeling the Great One opening as every moment and everything you do, and not get bound in patterns of self-reflection, needing an other—a *seeming* other—to love you, distracted in sex, afraid of death."

Mykonos's words arose in the silence, striking my deepest heart-knowing, and vanished. Their force continued to ring, soundlessly, appearing as everything, the shimmering grass, the trees, the monkeys. No separation spaced between my mind, his words, and all that appeared in the world. A deep and infinite wholeness bloomed outward, his words revealing depth's truth, and time relaxed wide open. Happening ceased to enfold. Just like gazing into the eyes of Mykonos's teacher, all opened without a crease or event of self-curl.

"No experience or knowledge exceeds this openness of love," Mykonos said. Then he turned to me and smiled.

"Have you seen my new chainsaw?" he asked.

"No."

"C'mon, I'll show it to you."

As we walked to the tool shed, the pattern of time was a soft breeze, and I could feel Mykonos smiling, although I could not see his face.

13
Burden of Bliss

It was my birthday and also the last day before Mykonos would be leaving the country to see his teacher. Mykonos suggested that we go to a favorite bar of his near the beach. Paco, Lemuel, Mykonos, and I met at the front door of the bar—dark, grimy, and reeking of stale beer and cigarettes—and we entered, sitting at a small table. Before meeting Mykonos, I couldn't have imagined being in such a place.

"Now there's a fine whoor," Mykonos said, looking toward a young woman behind the bar. Her skin was dark, her hair black and long. She was probably from India, or possibly Iran. She was beautiful.

"Well, my friends, this is it," Mykonos said, pouring beer from the pitcher we had ordered. "Have we done it?"

Paco raised his glass of beer. "Mykonos, I want to thank you for everything you've given us. This has been the most incredible time of my life. I wish you didn't have to go."

"To the Great One," Mykonos toasted.

"To the Great One," we all replied, drinking.

"Paco, are you going to be able to keep your friends happy?" Mykonos asked.

"I think so," Paco answered, smiling, getting Mykonos's joke.

"You're a good man, Paco. You have a great heart. Maybe one day you will learn how to use it," Mykonos laughed, putting his hand on Paco's shoulder. "Just kidding, my friend."

The dark-skinned woman from behind the bar appeared at our table.

"Can I get you anything else?" she asked.

"How about a few more pitchers?" Lemuel suggested.

"Sure, I'll bring them right away," she answered, and walked back behind the bar.

"Gentlemen, look around you," Mykonos suggested.

Most of the people in the bar were in their 50's or 60's. Some of the men had gray beards and large bellies. The women were older, too, with heavy make-up around their eyes. Almost everybody was smoking. At the table closest to us sat a man and a woman in their 50's, both quite heavy, wearing jeans, boots, and black leather jackets over T-shirts, probably bikers. At one table were two young men, almost certainly surfers. Except for the surfers, most people were sitting quietly, shifting their positions now and then, smoking and drinking, occasionally talking in quiet tones. The surfers were speaking loudly and laughing with each other.

"This human realm is not about happiness," Mykonos said, "unless you *locate* happiness, feeling the openness, the living play of the Great One—breathing love, giving love, living as love—in every moment. Otherwise, you are no different than these fuckers sitting around us, trying their best to get through the day, through their lives, not quite happy, resigned to the little comforts they've managed to hold onto."

I was not comfortable in that bar. I would rather have been outside on the beach in the late-afternoon sun, or swimming in the cool ocean water. I wore shorts and sandals just in case. But as Mykonos spoke, I practiced what I had learned from him, feeling the openness that was the place of every moment, breathing love as the substance of the moment, opening as the deep space of consciousness in which this *room* appeared.

Still, I didn't like the smoke and filth—every time my hand rested on the sticky table surface or my toes touched the grimy floor I would cringe—but, as I practiced, my deep heart relaxed. Relaxing open, breathing open, feeling open, my sensations—including discomfort—as well as my thoughts and the whole barroom were obviously alive as the Great One. An exquisite bliss permeated everything.

"Where are the ladies?" Mykonos asked.

"I told Michelle and Layla to come by after they got off work," Lemuel said.

Gia was out of town visiting her parents. Rebecca had returned to her home and job to take a pause and decide what she really wanted to do with her life, while Gia and I continued opening as well as we could through the painful unfurling and voluntary dissolution of our relationship's assumed form, practicing to offer our deepest hearts—to each other and the world—without depending on phantom resolution.

"Erin is spending tonight with her daughter," said Paco, "and I think Zelda is out on a date."

"And Dimitri?" Mykonos asked.

"He couldn't decide whether to go to a movie or meet us here. I guess he went to a movie," Lemuel answered.

The woman from behind the bar came with another pitcher of beer.

"Thank you very much, my dear," Mykonos said to her. "And how are you doing this evening?"

"Fine," she answered.

"Do you know Shiva?" Mykonos asked.

The waitress was startled. I was startled. Mykonos's question about the Hindu god Shiva seemed rather out of place.

"Yes," the barmaid answered.

"Mm-hmm. I thought you might. I can feel Shiva in your heart."

The barmaid's face grew distraught. She walked away with quick steps, disappearing through a door near the bar.

"That whoor is suffering. She doesn't want to be here," Mykonos said quietly.

She had seemed a little sad—but everyone in the bar, except the surfers, seemed glum. The bar itself was rundown. The barmaid's sadness didn't seem so out of place.

"Always bring happiness to a woman's heart, gentlemen," Mykonos said, looking suddenly heartbroken himself.

I remembered a story Mykonos once told me about his first few days in Vietnam. His platoon was on patrol when they came to a Viet Cong village. The sergeant rounded up all the women and children—there were no men—and forced them into a bunker. The platoon sergeant—Mykonos called him Sergeant Rhodes—wouldn't allow the women to leave their babies outside.

As Mykonos told me this story, he seemed more vulnerable than I had ever felt him. His expression turned fragile, and he seemed to be in another place as the words came from his lips. I'll never forget Mykonos's description of that horrible event.

"Rhodes took a drag off his cigarette," Mykonos said, his eyes gazing into a scene from thirty years earlier as if it were before him now. "Then, he pulled a hand grenade from his ammunition belt, yanked the ring, and tossed it into the bunker. And then another grenade.

"I heard two muffled explosions. White smoke poured out of the bunker."

Mykonos said that he went numb, and then he wanted to kill Sergeant Rhodes. Mykonos had his finger on the trigger of his rifle, when a fellow soldier stopped him, telling him it was too late.

The sergeant went on to slaughter other innocent people during Mykonos's time in his platoon. The only regret I ever heard in Mykonos's voice was when he told me about not killing Rhodes.

"If it weren't for women, what kind of place would this be?" Mykonos asked.

Paco raised his beer and toasted, "To women!"

Mykonos raised his beer, but did not smile.

Over the next hour or so, I walked up to the bar a few times to order more pitchers, since the barmaid didn't return to our table. We were getting fairly drunk.

Two girls had joined the surfers at their table.

"Happy birthday, my friend," Mykonos said to me. "Do you know what you have to do?"

Mykonos's question touched me at so many levels that for a moment I froze in confusion. But feeling penetrated by the deep black of his eyes, all possibilities resolved into a singular depth of knowing. I was certain of what I had to do—in that moment, and for the rest of my life.

"Yes," I answered.

"Good," Mykonos replied. "Do we have any cigarettes?"

I had brought a pack of cigarettes and a lighter, anticipating Mykonos might want to smoke. I gave him a cigarette. He put it in between his lips, and I lit it. Again he looked into my eyes, briefly, while he took the first puff.

I already missed Mykonos.

"Ma!" Mykonos shouted, as the barmaid walked near our table. "Ma, come over here."

The barmaid reluctantly walked to our table, but stood a little farther away than before.

"It's our friend's birthday here. Would you join us and sing Happy Birthday to him?" Mykonos asked.

"No thanks," the barmaid answered, looking down at the beer-stained floor.

"That's fine," Mykonos said. "Do you miss Mother India?"

The barmaid's head jerked up. She looked at Mykonos. She nodded yes.

"But you can feel Shiva in your heart, can't you ma?" Mykonos asked. "Hmmm?"

Tears filled the barmaid's eyes as she continued looking at Mykonos.

Everything else in the bar seemed to disappear. She and he held their gaze as the rest of the world faded into white. The scene was out of time, ancient. The two could have been anywhere, in a desert, a temple, a cave. The barmaid stood before Mykonos, his eyes on fire with pain, with love, speaking the woman's deepest heart aloud.

"It's OK, ma," Mykonos continued. "Shiva is here, too. It's OK to love him."

The barmaid stood transfixed, unblinking, her lips aquiver, her fingers rigid. Slowly, through the tears, she smiled, and relaxed. She was so radiant, so defenseless, so exposed.

And softly, tenderly, Mykonos: "How about another pitcher of beer, ma?"

The barmaid smiled and nodded. Before walking from the table she bowed her head to Mykonos just slightly, almost unnoticeably.

"A *very* fine whoor," Mykonos said, looking as if he had just said goodbye to his beloved.

"Hi guys!" Layla said as she bounced from the door over to our table. She and Michelle were all dressed up, wearing high heels and black skirts. Layla was wearing a colorful blouse and Michelle was wearing a black bra under a see-through top.

"Wow!" Mykonos exclaimed, smiling, appreciatively looking Layla and Michelle up and down. "I'm glad you two could make it."

Paco poured them beers, and we all talked and drank. The barmaid never returned to our table.

"Michelle, you look like you're out to get laid tonight," Mykonos said.

"Well, it's been a while," she said.

"What's the longest you've gone without cock?" Mykonos asked Michelle.

"What do you mean? Lately?"

"As an adult. Since you've been sexual."

"I don't now, it varies. I guess I've gone several months without sex, but I started having sex when I was twelve years old," Michelle said.

"How about you, Layla, when did you first get laid?" Mykonos asked.

"I was seventeen. Just before I went to college."

"Mm-hmm. Look around this room, ladies. Is this how you want to end up?"

Layla and Michelle looked around the bar. It was truly a downtrodden place. Michelle looked at the biker couple sitting near us. The woman's hair was gray, her lipstick was bright red, and her face was lined and weathered. The skin around her lips was pleated, probably from years of smoking. Her man was drinking his beer and looking around the bar. She was stoking the back of his hand, when he wasn't lifting it to drink beer.

"I hope I don't end up sitting in a place like this when I'm that age," Michelle said.

"You are sitting here right now," Mykonos pointed out.

"Yeah, but we're here for a reason," said Michelle.

"So are they," said Mykonos.

"What are you trying to say, Mykonos?" asked Layla.

"I'm trying to say there is more to life than getting laid."

"Look who's talking," Layla said.

"Do you want to end up planting your fat ass on a barstool for the rest of your life, clinging to some dipshit guy who buys your beer?" Mykonos asked.

"Mykonos, that will never happen to me," Layla said.

"Layla, my dear, you might end up married to a handsome aristocrat, living in a mansion, shitting on white doilies, but deep inside, your heart is going to feel just like that woman's over there, unless you learn to love larger than the *room* you grew up in. What about you, Michelle?" Mykonos asked.

"What about me?"

"Is all you care about circumscribed by that little pussy of yours?"

"What do you mean?"

"Let me ask you a question. If there was a line of 1008 men outside, standing naked, all with erections, and the man in the middle was playing a big drum, which one would you fuck?"

"I'd fuck them all! Why fuck just one?"

"Yes," Mykonos said laughing. "I think you would. How about a line of silverback gorillas? Have you ever seen the look in a silverback's eyes? They are so peaceful, so humble, yet majestic and noble. They are dying—we are killing them, killing them all—and they know it. Would you rather fuck a silverback, or, say, one of those guys at that table?" Mykonos asked, nodding his head toward the surfers.

"Oh, I'd fuck a silverback for sure," Michelle answered.

"Exactly," Mykonos said.

"I still don't know what you're talking about," Layla complained.

"We are all dying. Everybody is dying," Mykonos said forcefully, "and yet this is the vision of God. This, right here. Ladies, will you consent to open your hearts?"

"I'm going to the bathroom," Layla said, and walked off.

"I'll be right back," Michelle said, following Layla.

"Don't you love women?" Mykonos asked us.

Paco was looking at the blonde woman sitting with the surfers and didn't answer.

Lemuel said, "Yup."

Then Mykonos turned and looked right into my eyes. He was crying. I had never seen Mykonos cry before.

He grabbed my ears in his two hands and pulled me close to his face.

"You have been given a burden of bliss," Mykonos said quietly, but with absolute intention. "You know what you have to do."

I nodded.

"Happy birthday," Mykonos said, and kissed me on the lips. "This burden is my gift to you."

Mykonos sat back and looked out over all the people in the barroom. His open eyes glistened. I knew I would not be seeing him again for a long time—maybe I wouldn't be seeing him again at all.

Layla and Michelle returned and we continued drinking and talking for about an hour, but I felt lodged in a place not quite coincident with the *room*. Mykonos never looked into my eyes again. When rain began to fall outside, the night felt over.

"Well, have we done it?" Mykonos asked.

"Yes," we all answered.

Layla and Michelle hugged us, said their goodbyes to Mykonos, and left in Layla's car.

Lemuel, Paco, Mykonos, and I walked out into the parking lot. The day had been hot, and now the rain felt warm.

Paco started weeping. "I'm going to miss you, Mykonos."

Paco put one of his arms around Mykonos's shoulder and the other around Lemuel. I joined in the huddle, arms around my friends. We were standing in the rain, embracing in a circle, spending one last moment together.

Then, I realized that Mykonos was pissing on my foot, in the warm rain.

ABOUT THE AUTHOR

Acknowledged as one of the world's most insightful and provocative spiritual teachers of our time, best-selling author **David Deida** continues to revolutionize the way that men and women grow spiritually and sexually. His teaching and writing on a radically practical spirituality for our time have been hailed as among the most original and authentic contributions to personal and spiritual growth currently available.

Deida is known worldwide as the author of over 70 books, audiotapes, essays, and articles that bring to light a fully integral approach to spirituality. His books include: *Finding God Through Sex; The Way of the Superior Man; Dear Lover; Wild Nights; The Way of the Superior Lover; Intimate Communion; It's a Guy Thing;* and the recently released *Naked Buddhism.*

He is a founding associate of Integral Institute and has taught and conducted research at the University of California Medical School in San Diego; University of California, Santa Cruz; San Jose State University; Lexington Institute, Boston; and *Ecole Polytechnique* in Paris, France.

Deida presents his integral program for spiritual awakening through writing and working with people internationally, offering workshops, seminars, intensives, and professional trainings for men and women who are ready to move beyond the therapeutic model of popular personal growth regimes. Through his teaching and writing, Deida speaks directly to the heart of love and freedom that is the spiritual source of every man and woman's being.

To order books and audiotapes, or for more information about David Deida's work and a current teaching schedule, call toll-free:

1-888-MAN-WOMAN
(1-888-626-9662)
(outside the US: +1 512.349-0599 or email info@deida.com)

or visit the deida.com website at:
www.deida.com
[teaching schedule, unpublished essays, articles, book and tape excerpts, community, and much more]

BOOKS BY DAVID DEIDA

Naked Buddhism
39 Ways to Free Your Heart and Awaken to Now
Foreword by LAMA SURYA DAS

"The openness, the love! What lively new language David Deida finds for the unsayable!"
—**Coleman Barks**
Author of *The Essential Rumi*

"...a brilliant book, absolutely gorgeous. ...Deida has reached a new level of poetic genius in his writing... I am just knocked out by this book."
—**Miranda Shaw Ph.D.**
Author of *Passionate Enlightenment: Women in Tantric Buddhism*

Softcover, 210 p. $16.95

Dear Lover
A Woman's Guide to Enjoying Love's Deepest Bliss
Foreword by MARIANNE WILLIAMSON

Dear Lover is David Deida's long-awaited guide written especially for women on sacred intimacy and spiritual growth through love, sexuality, and intimate relationship.

"Listen with me to the wizard of romance. He speaks to us of a long lost promise. He speaks of truth. He speaks of Love."
—From the foreword by **Marianne Williamson**

Softcover, 210 p. $16.95

Finding God Through Sex
A Spiritual Guide to Ecstatic Loving and Deep Passion for Men and Women
Foreword by KEN WILBER

"We all taste God, taste Goddess, taste pure Spirit in those moments of sexual rapture, and wise men and women have always used that rapture to reveal Spirit's innermost secrets. David Deida is such a wise one. David's language is a model of evocative spirituality. Let the richness of your heart unfold in the gentle invitations...swoon into that radiant light that is your own true nature. The secrets to all of this are given in the following pages, so let the passionate adventure in sexual spirituality begin..."
—From the foreword by **Ken Wilber**

Softcover, 320 p. $18.95

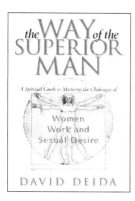

The Way of the Superior Man
A Spiritual Guide to Mastering the Challenges of Women, Work, and Sexual Desire

"*The Way of the Superior Man* is quite wonderful. Finally, a guide for the noncastrated male. To transcend the body-mind means to transcend and include its sexuality, not transcend and evaporate it. Few are the books that discuss strong sexuality within strong spirituality, instead of tepid sexuality diluted by a mediocre spiritual stance. This book steps straightforwardly into the challenge."
—**Ken Wilber**
Author of *A Theory of Everything*

Hardcover, 256 p. $23.95

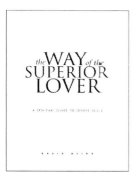

The Way of the Superior Lover
A Spiritual Guide to Sexual Skills

Many readers have found this practical guide to be a useful companion to *Finding God Through Sex*. This book covers spiritual sexuality in detail, including: Breath and the circulation of sexual energy; Bypassing ejaculation; Multiple whole-body orgasms for women AND MEN; The three main types of women's orgasms; Sexual variations beyond the taboo; Retraining your nervous system to conduct maximum sexual pleasure; Conscious circulation of sexual energy between partners; Using heightened sexual energy as a sacramental prayer of love; much more.

Spiral Bound $29.95

Waiting to Love
Rude Essays on Life After Spirituality

These stunning essays offer the fire of real love, spontaneous liberation, and lasting transformation. Dive into the flames with Deida and find out who you really are.

"*Waiting to Love* takes us into the wide uncharted waters of true self-discovery. David Deida is one of the most courageous pioneers at the cutting edge of spiritual life."
—**Arjuna Ardagh**
Author of *How About Now?*

"An amazing and truly great work—Art. I've never seen anything vaguely like it."
—**Terry Patten**
Author of *Blowback: Technology's Hidden Consequences*

Softcover, 250 p. $16.95

TO ORDER NOW, PLEASE CALL PLEXUS TOLL-FREE
1-888-626-9662 OR VISIT OUR WEBSITE WWW.DEIDA.COM

Intimate Communion
Awakening Your Sexual Essence

David Deida's first book, *Intimate Communion* lays down many of the basic principles of his teaching on the integration of spirituality and sexuality. It is filled with practical understandings that will immediately help you to turn your intimacy and all your relationships into sacred, ecstatic celebrations of your deepest heart.

"Intimate Communion is a major contribution to the exploration of male and female spirituality."
—**Craig Schindler, J.D., Ph.D.**
Author of *The Great Turning*
President of *Project Victory*

Softcover, 270 p. $11.95

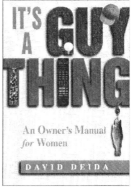

It's A Guy Thing
An Owner's Manual for Women

David Deida brings his customary deep insight and unconventional perspectives to over 150 of women's most asked questions about men and intimacy.

Hailed as an invaluable contribution toward increased understanding between the sexes, *It's a Guy Thing* is David's most accessible book to date.

Softcover, 260 p. $11.95

Men's Challenge Deck
Practicing The Way of the Superior Man
by Rob Biagini

Based on David Deida's bestseller—*The Way of the Superior Man*—The Men's Challenge Deck is a tool for men's personal and spiritual growth in men's groups. Each of the 80 cards offers a challenge for a man to carry out—either alone or with others—that will help him clarify his deepest life purpose and give his fullest gifts in each moment.

"I highly recommend this insightful tool."
—**John Lee**
Author of *The Flying Boy*

Card Deck, Booklet $34.95

**TO ORDER NOW, PLEASE CALL PLEXUS TOLL-FREE
1-888-626-9662 OR VISIT OUR WEBSITE WWW.DEIDA.COM**

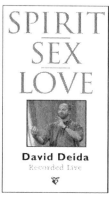

VIDEO: Spirit Sex Love *David Deida Recorded Live*

This rare live video footage of David Deida working with participants in seminars on sexual spirituality is lively, humorous, provocative, deeply insightful, and filled with practical understandings and wisdom that will inspire men and women to live from the deep source of their hearts and give their fullest gifts in intimacy and beyond. The video includes live footage of David Deida's workshops, interviews with David, and interviews with couples from workshops.

This first available video of David Deida has been a long time coming, but we're sure that you will agree that it's been worth the wait for this professionally produced, broadcast-quality debut. Great as either an introduction to David's work on spiritual intimacy or as an inspiring refresher course for more advanced practitioners, you will watch *Spirit Sex Love* over and over again.

David Deida
Recorded Live

VHS, 85 min. $29.95

AUDIO* BY DAVID DEIDA

Living Sacred Intimacy
Two Cassettes $19.95 or Two CDs $24.95
This audio set (either two audiocasstes or two CDs) gives you a complete introduction to David Deida's work in spirituality, sexuality, and intimacy. Including an exploration of the three stages of human spiritual and sexual evolution; living from your core sexual essence; our masculine and feminine "shells"; working with jealousy and anger; finding masculine purpose; attracting the intimate partner we most deeply desire; boundaries and attachment; and much more.

Living The Third Stage Series
Six Cassettes $129.95
The uniqueness of David Deida's teaching is his focus on growing beyond dependence (first stage), and beyond independence (second stage), to the moment-by-moment magnification of love and consciousness that is living in and from the third stage. The tapes in the "Living The Third Stage" series explore the realm of human existence from the third stage point of view.

Volume 1: The Three Stages of Life
Volume 2: The Play of Masculine and Feminine
Volume 3: Communication, Yearning, and Purpose
Volume 4: Primary Emotion and Deep Purpose
Volume 5: Realms of Love and Substance
Volume 6: Trusting Larger Than Yourself

The Nuts & Bolts of Spiritual Intimacy
Three 90-min. Cassettes $29.95
David Deida—recorded live in Telluride, CO in August 1999—speaking on the differences between masculine and feminine spirituality and the moment-to-moment practice of using intimacy as a means of spiritual growth. This series of talks and Q&A provides a very thorough understanding of how to create and nourish a spiritual intimacy. Sexual, emotional, and spiritual practices for both men and women are covered in detail.

Go to **WWW.DEIDA.COM to order MP3 CDs containing **ALL** of David Deida's available audio recordings!*

Living Dialogs with David Deida & Duncan Campbell, 2 *Cassettes $19.95*
Noted interviewer Duncan Campbell and David Deida explore the philosophical and cultural context of Deida's work on the three developmental stages of individual and social evolution and how the universal masculine and feminine energies play out in the human realm through those stages. Includes a fascinating discussion about what it takes to make real use of a spiritual teacher and the limits of ethical and moral responsibility in the guru-disciple relationship.

At Your Edge: Spiritual and Sexual Wisdom for Men, 2 *Cassettes, $19.95*
Freedom, power, fear, money, sex, enlightenment, death, wisdom, excellence, challenge, transcendence, purpose—living at your edge is the masculine form of spiritual practice. No man is truly happy unless he is living a life of facing his fears and transcending them in his quest to give the gift he was born to give. In these tapes, David Deida lays down in crystal clear terms what it takes to live a masculine life of integrity, authenticity, and depth.

BINGO: The Practice of Boundless Love, *One Cassette, 90 min. $12.95*
This tape explores the practice of opening beyond our self-made boundaries into a "BINGO" moment where we recognize each other and all as one heart of love and boundless freedom. This tape explores common obstructions to BINGO and ways of practicing openness in the midst of those obstructions.

Spirituality Beyond Self Improvement, *One Cassette, 100 min. $12.95*
Self improvement is a good thing, but all the self-mastery and personal growth in the world don't add up to real spiritual openness. And neither does true spiritual openness depend on being a well-adjusted, "successful" person. In this intimate Q&A session, David Deida explores the limits of self improvement, therapy, and personal growth and clarifies the process of real heart opening spiritual practice.

The Yoga of Deep Passion, *One Cassette, 90 min. $12.95*
In this tape, David Deida explores a variety of topics, from the neurotic "shells" of sexual energy that cover our core sexual essence, to working with anger, the roots of romantic attraction, and the nature of all appearance as the moment-by-moment sexual union of consciousness (the masculine principle) and radiance (the feminine principle). Along the way, he clarifies how living the fullest sexual life that we can requires a spiritual commitment to our own deep passion.

Q&A at Breitenbush, 1999, *One Cassette, 90 min. $12.95*
Topics covered in this lively, humorous Q&A include: Why dark sexual energy is important; Maintaining sexual passion for couples who work together; Dealing with sexual energy in the workplace; Who women should be open with and when; How men can find their deep purpose and live from it; and much more...

Intimacy to Ecstasy, *One Cassette, 70 min. $12.95*
This interview with David Deida, conducted by noted radio host Alan Hutner, is an excellent introduction to the basics of David's teaching on the integration of spirituality and sexuality.

Questions in the Philosophy of Spiritual Practice:
David Deida interviewed by Vartman, *One Cassette, 90 min. $12.95*
Author and Advaita Vedanta spiritual teacher Vartman interviews David Deida on a variety of topics in the philosophy of spiritual practice. Includes a discussion on why bothering to practice spiritually at all, the stages of practice that people grow through, and specific questions about the practices that Deida recommends in his workshops.

Opening As Love and Nothingness, *One Cassette, 60 min. $12.95*
The infinite openness of no separation, or oneness, is the spiritual truth of every moment. On our way to unobstructed realization of that truth, we tend to seek it in two very different ways. Some of us (those who are more feminine in their core) open toward infinite oneness as love. Some of us (those who are more masculine in their core) open toward that same oneness as "nothingness". In this tape, David Deida explores these two different paths of opening, how they interact with each other, and the gesture of practicing opening more and more in each present moment.

Love, Fear, Trust, and Depth, *One Cassette, 60 min. $12.95*
Fear often restricts intimate partners from growing in love and trust. Moving beyond fear into open love invites trust, just as trust invites open love. In this presentation, David Deida reveals how men can invite their women to open in love, and how women can invite their men to become more trustable. He also discusses how to choose an intimate partner for those who are not currently in a relationship.

Opening Spiritually and Sexually, *One Cassette, 110 min. $12.95*
Opening spiritually and opening sexually are the same thing. And the personal "kinks" that close us down sexually also close us down to deep spiritual experience. In this humorous, wide ranging introduction to spiritual and sexual practice, David Deida explores the fundamental gesture of opening to real bliss and spiritual depth in every moment, under all circumstances.

The Love That Washes Through Patterns, *One Cassette, 100 min. $12.95*
"If you are in a good relationship, the worst, hellish stuff that you're ever going to face is going to come up." With these sobering words, David Deida goes on to describe and lead workshop participants through practices of love that transform those patterns of behavior which limit our intimacies, popping us through the patterns to the ecstasy of love-bliss that lies waiting on the other side.

The Shiva & Shakti Scales: Our Search for Love & Freedom, *80 min. $12.95*
Shiva and Shakti are Hindu terms for the masculine and feminine aspects of the divine. In this deeply insightful talk, David Deida explores the full spectrums of the universal masculine and feminine energies from dark to light, showing why it is essential that each of us embrace the full spectrum in order to liberate our fullest love, energy, and presence for our spiritual growth.

Kinks, Consciousness, & the Plumber, *One Cassette, 70 min. $12.95*
Talks on the embodiment of spiritual practice in love and intimacy. A rare peek inside what has been called one of the most transformative workshop experiences available.

Rested Deeper Than Habit, *One Cassette, 90 min. $12.95*
Habits. Perhaps the biggest single obstruction to our growth as spiritual beings are the unconscious habits and patterns of thought, behavior, experience, and relationship that we develop and settle into in our lives. Recognizing the deep source of who we are "behind" or "beneath" or "before" our habits and patterns is a primary foundation of spiritual practice.

His Freedom, Her Love, *One Cassette, 70 min. $12.95*
David Deida recorded live during a workshop in Byron Bay, Australia in July of 2000. In each of us is a masculine principle or force that is always searching for more freedom. And in each of us is a feminine principle or force that is always searching for more love. These two different expressions of our sexual core are each fundamental aspects of an understanding of spiritual growth as sexual beings. In this tape, David Deida explores spiritual practice as the search for freedom and love.

TO ORDER NOW, PLEASE CALL PLEXUS TOLL-FREE 1-888-626-9662 OR VISIT OUR WEBSITE WWW.DEIDA.COM

ORDER FORM

To order call toll-free **1-888-626-9662**
PLEXUS 815-A Brazos #445, Austin, TX 78701

NAME ....
 PLEASE PRINT ALL INFORMATION

ADDRESS ....
 BILLING ADDRESS IF PAYING BY CREDIT CARD

CITY .... **PHONE** ....

STATE/PROVINCE .... **ZIP/POSTAL** ....
 IF SHIPPING TO A DIFFERENT ADDRESS, PLEASE INCLUDE ON A A SEPARATE SHEET

PAYMENT METHOD: ❑ CHECK*   ❑ VISA / MASTERCARD / AMEX

CARD # _ _ _ _ | _ _ _ _ | _ _ _ _ | _ _ _ _   EXP. _ _ / _ _

SIGNATURE ....
 *CHECKS OR MONY ORDERS MUST BE MADE PAYABLE IN US FUNDS DRAWN ON A US BANK

ITEM	QTY	PRICE	TOTAL

SHIPPING CHARGES

	FIRST ITEM	ADDTL ITEMS
USA / CANADA	$5.00	$2.50
ASIA / EUROPE	$11.00	$7.50

⬅

SUBTOTAL

TEXAS RESIDENTS ONLY 6.25% (AUSTIN 8.25%) **TAX**

SHIPPING & HANDLING

TOTAL

To order call toll-free **1-888-626-9662**
[INTL. +1 512 349 0599]
or mail this form to:
PLEXUS 815-A Brazos #445, Austin, TX 78701

ORDER SECURELY ON THE WEB AT
WWW.DEIDA.COM